CW00544925

Subjects and Sequences:
a Margaret Tait reader

Edited by Peter Todd and Benjamina Cook

Published by LUX

Subjects and Sequences:
a Margaret Tait reader
Edited by Peter Todd and Benjamin Cook

Published in Great Britain 2004 by
LUX, 3rd Floor, 18 Shacklewell Lane, London E8 2EZ
www.lux.org.uk

© the individual authors, Alex Pirie and LUX, 2004

All rights reserved. No part of this book may be reproduced, stored
in a retrieval system, or transmitted in any form, by any means,
including mechanical, electronic, photocopying, recording or
otherwise, without prior written permission of the publishers.

Every effort has been made to trace the copyright holders, but if any
has been inadvertently overlooked the publisher will be pleased to
make the necessary arrangements at the first opportunity.

Designed by Sarah Wood
Printed in the Netherlands by Lecturis

ISBN 0 954 85690 2

A catalogue record for this book is available from the British Library.

Contents

Introduction
PETER TODD   1

Essays, interviews
The Margaret Tait years
ALI SMITH   7

Where I am is here: a patchwork for Margaret Tait
A celebration, an argument, some voices
GARETH EVANS   35

Margaret Tait: marks of time
LUCY REYNOLDS   57

In her own words
selected by DAVID CURTIS   77

Preserving the Margaret Tait Film Collection
JANET McBAIN and ALAN RUSSELL   101

Poems, stories, texts
selected by SARAH WOOD and PETER TODD   117

Resources
Chronology   149
Filmography   158
Bibliography   170
Resources   174
Contributors   176

Portrait of Margaret Tait c.1936

Introduction

One of the retrospective screenings in this year's
Edinburgh Festival is for a Scottish film-maker. Much
of Margaret Tait's work has never before been publicly
shown. For twenty years this independent artist, who
is also a poet and painter, has in fact been quietly
achieving the impossible, that is turning out over
fifteen films without financial backing from anyone and
with no clear prospect of getting them shown. In the
process she has not surprisingly developed a highly
individual style uncompromised by outside pressures,
commercial or otherwise.
— Elizabeth Sussex, *Financial Times*,
9 September 1970.

Thirty-four years later and Margaret Tait is again the subject
of a retrospective at the Edinburgh International Film
Festival. This is the result of growing interest in her work.
I had been including her films that were in distribution, in
programmes which toured nationally and also screened
abroad. Over a number of years, my work has been, in part, a

dialogue between making films and screening films. Margaret was supportive of this process. I have been developing programmes exploring the relationship between film and poetry, *Film Poems* (www.lux.org.uk/filmpoems), and also the programmes exploring how gardens and landscape have been filmed, *Garden Pieces*, which took its name from her last film, and *Trees Plants Flowers – Lives*. Most of these programmes had one or two of her films in them alongside works by Bruce Baillie, Stan Brakhage, Maya Deren, Rose Lowder, Guy Sherwin and myself, amongst others. Margaret and I had corresponded and discussed thoughts for a programme on animation and painting on film.

When Margaret died, I organised a tribute screening at the LUX cinema in London. In partnership with LUX, Scottish Screen Archive, and her husband, Alex Pirie, I sought to ensure that Margaret's films would be preserved, and made available for screening. Because Margaret's books (three volumes of poetry and two of short stories) remain hard to find, we have included a small selection of her work here. There is still much to be achieved: paper material catalogued, further films preserved, a collected poems published.

It is perhaps a reflection on cinema today that those interested in Margaret Tait's films are often those involved in art and literature. In the second century of cinema, Margaret Tait's work reminds us of what cinema is and can be. Cinema can be personal. Films can be revisited, just like returning to a novel or re-reading a poem. Films can be made over several years. Films can be made in the country. Cinema can take place in venues such as village halls, a room in a house, in a garden, in galleries, and in small groups with talk or discussion and in cinemas of all shape, size and type.

Screen the films. Look at the films.

August 2004

Stills from the films of Margaret Tait

Portrait of Margaret Tait c.1992

Essays, interviews

Still, *Aspects of Kirkwall: Some Changes*

The Margaret Tait years

Why are there no poems by Margaret Tait included in the (most definitive so far) volume of *Modern Scottish Women Poets* published by Canongate in 2003?

Why, when you ask most literate film and book lovers, including people in Scotland, even in the north of Scotland, have they heard of Margaret Tait, do they look distant and shake their heads?

Why did I, as a reasonably well-read Highlander myself, a person who grew up in the Highlands and studied Scottish literature alongside other literatures, and as someone who has been seeking out all sorts and genres of books and all sorts and genres of films and art all my life, only come across my first Margaret Tait poems and films as recently as two or three years ago?

Because things slip away from us all the time.

Because that's what time is, things slipping away from us.

Because Tait published her own poems at the end of the fifties and beginning of the sixties in three finely made, beautiful, slim little collections marked with her trademark heartbeat, the graphic sign of life – and these are collections which are now, understandably, quite hard to find. (Her poetry has been totally critically ignored. Someone should publish a Collected Tait, illustrated with stills from her films.)

Because she made films that were nothing to do with the film market, so unless you sought them out, tipped off by a good and clever friend, you'd have a hard time finding them.

Because women artists do tend, historically, to get lost more easily, to fall off the back off the canonical.

Margaret Tait knew that things, lives, art, are lost to us all the time, in the same way that her own films were made of a material that rots and self-implodes. It's one of the recurring themes in her films, one of the concerns of her poetry, but it's not a personal concern, her work is much less selfish than this. What characterises her poetry and her films, instead, is empathy, an openness to the moment of being alive and to the life of things beyond and synchronic with the self, and an honesty at one level brusque and at another near-brutal, keen to shake things apart to see how things are put together:

It's the looking that matters,
The being prepared to see what there is to see...
Botanically detaching petals that maybe should
    be left alone
And roughly shattering things, too, to see
    what's there.
— Margaret Tait, "Seeing's Believing and Believing's Seeing", "Margaret Tait Film Maker 1918–1999: Indications Influence Outcomes", 1958–59

The very first poem of Tait's first book, *Origins and Elements*, correctly redefines the word elastic as something that can return to its original shape after being stretched. A combination of elasticity and toughness makes for a gruff *joie de vivre* in her poetic voice, as she goes on through the collection to redefine concepts of heaven, hell, nationhood, art, sex, gender, the elemental and scientific worlds. Her poetic tone is notably conversational, her poetic line is breath-length, part of her poetry's willingness – more, its demand that things be discursive and open. Her poems practically act out the act of thinking – often that's what one of her poems is, an intelligent probing, a thought or thoughts followed through to what's generally an open end. There's a battle in her poems between human warmth and existentialism; this battle is evident in her films too. As both poet and film maker, she makes difficult demands; it is hard, to have identity flung open.

> I didn't want you cosy and neat and limited.
> I didn't want you to be understandable,
> Understood.
> I wanted you to stay mad and limitless,
> Neither bound to me nor bound to anyone else's or
>   your own preconceived idea of yourself.
> — Margaret Tait, "To Anybody At All",
> *Origins and Elements,* 1959

Her poetry refuses preconception and sees pretence as immoral and fearful. "Something in people that prefers falseness. / It's fear, I suppose, / Fear of the real, / Fear they may not be equal to it." In fact, according to Tait, "the wilful denial / Of one's own consciousness" is a kind of death, and so is a refusal to engage openly, to "respond to each moment".

In her small body of published poems she urges us to see, emphasises the responsibility of the artist to see, and strives, in this argumentative, stubborn, elasticity of voice, for a widened sense of understanding, meaning, independent vision.

Tait was a remarkable critical forerunner in her poetry of what's now a recognisable Scottish literary voice, one that took ten or twenty years after her own publications to come to the fore in newer voices credited with kick-starting the late twentieth-century renaissance in Scottish writing. She's a writer whose openness of mind, voice, structure, all come from the Beats and Whitman crossed with MacDiarmid, but then cut their own original (and crucially female) path. She is a unique and underrated film maker. Born of the Italian neorealists, formed of her own Scottish pragmatism, Highland lyricism, optimism, generosity and experimental spirit, she is a forerunner of the British experimental directors of the later twentieth-century. She is a clear pioneer of the poetic, the experimental and the democratic traditions, in the best of risk-taking Scottish cinema. Put another way, Margaret Tait knows how to cross a good border.

The contradictory and paradoxical thing is that in a documentary the real things depicted are liable to lose their reality by being photographed and presented in that 'documentary' way, and there's no poetry in that. In poetry, something else happens. Hard to say what it is. Presence, let's say, soul or spirit, an empathy with whatever it is that's dwelt upon, feeling for it – to the point of identification.

— "Film-poem or poem-film: A Few Notes about Film and Poetry", *Poem Film Film Poem*, No. 2, 1997

1992. Finally, in her seventies, Tait was able to make her first feature film, from a script she'd been working on since the 1940s.

Blue Black Permanent ought to have been the glorious culmination of a life's work. Instead, being a feature, and being shackled to the narrative demands of a feature script, it is a revelation of how far beyond standard narrative Tait has come, and how what people generally expect of a film narrative turns to a kind of artifice in her hands. The question at its centre is: what will survive of us? Its story, a past-present fusion, is a legacy of drowned lost women and it is one of Tait's bleakest visions, typically at its most powerful in its anti-narrative. Its interstices – the sense of psychological strangeness which arises from its artificial tone, its dream sequences, its city shots and shots of sea surfaces and depths – are its real narrative. "Press reaction in Scotland was dismissive," Alex Pirie writes. Its open unsolved ending is pure Tait, brave and radical and haunting, left in the air.

1981. In her sixties, by contrast, Tait made *Land Makar*.

A voice behind the image, the title written over and over itself in faint chalk, asks the film maker what the title means. It means poet of the land, the film maker (we presume) says. "Some beauty!" the woman's local voice says, ironic. But the first set of images are harvest images, footage of corn being stooked and gathered; hard work, and the colour gold. The voice-over is entirely local, local in the way that makes the ear remember what it is both to belong to a place and to not belong, to not be able to make out what exactly is being said. There's room for good-natured guesswork here, room for well-meaning understanding, in this film poem about landscape's gifts and landscape's structure, the structure of the seasons and the structure of survival.

Land Makar depends on chronology – Tait keeps chronology here because time and the seasons are what form both the woman working the farm and the landscape she works. So, after the harvest, there are ice shards on the reeds in the pond, there's a drift of smoke from a chimney across a still dusk sky. Then spring, and its new greens and yellows (because Tait as film maker is a pure eye for colour), then summer, then the wind getting up as autumn comes in, and winter, the end again before the next beginning. Within this chronology, from its start, there's the film's focus, a woman, on a tractor, and as soundtrack (rare for Tait) the real sound, the tractor engine. This film is about the work process. The voice-over soundtrack is a dialogue between the film maker, presumably, and the woman whose life the film is about. But they don't talk about film, they talk about weather, people, work, everything else.

Land Makar is a record of one person's dialogue with
landscape, the give and take between them, the farming of a
piece of ground which looks wild and unfarmable, but isn't,
has been given its shape. It's about how things keep their
fertile shape, and how we can, if we put in the steady work
and thought, make things give of themselves and be more
than themselves. It is above all about the dignity of this work.
The dialogue is everything; finally what we hear on the
soundtrack can be said to be the voice of the landscape, the
voice that's made it what it is and the voice that's been so
unsentimentally made by it. Some beauty! It's a paean to
survival, and, as usual, Tait finds the unforced image that
will tell its viewer everything. A roof, patched and holding,
even, as she pans along it, with great spreads of grass all
over it.

The haphazardness / the symmetry of a good standing dry
stone wall. A momentary symmetry of several ducks all
turning their heads in the same direction. The momentary,
haphazard symmetry is matched by Tait to the seasonal
symmetry, and the steadiness of it, the hard work of it, the
sparseness and richness of it, all revealed, calibrated,
celebrated, in a way that frees and marks both the spirit of
the woman and the spirit of the place. It becomes a dialogue
of spirits.

1976. In her late fifties, Margaret Tait edited her recording,
before she moved out of the house and it disappeared, of her
Place of Work.

Joyous music and joyous fast edits open this film in a play
of colour and shade, a loving brio of shots of her work table
piled with reels of film, her books, her work tools. The phone
rings. The film maker (we presume) answers it, we can hear
her in the background speaking into the air. Meanwhile the
camera continues to roam the room, settling on the peace and
the green out of the open door, then going for a walk as if by
itself, out to the garden to record the layering of living, the
things that happen round us while we're off doing something

else. Green space, birdsong, leaves on grass, the movement of light, as if to suggest that that's what work really is. The place of work, as happens so often in Tait's films, gives way to the garden. Men beyond it are roadworking – this film about the place of work in our lives has a strong heartbeat, the sound of one of the road-pounders outside the house. Tait loves tractors, bulldozers, machinery of all kinds (she loves to perch a tough old lady unexpectedly on a tractor, for instance, as she did in *Land Makar*); she likes filming machines almost as much as she likes filming dogs and cats – in a way she sees a common link between our relationships with machines and with domestic animals, an interlayering of usefulness, a willingness to get the job done.

The day comes down, the season turns. That's the film's structure, time-chronology, also often the Tait structure. Later this year Tait will finish making *Tailpiece*, a film about time and the passing of light, the camera trailing lightfall in the house, centring on an Edwardian-looking photo-portrait of a child on the wall, then on the reflection of the film maker herself, filming, then following, to a burst of 60s pop music, men emptying the house of its furniture. In her steady recording of incidental-seeming image and time, the small details of the margins, something simple and profound happens: time and place become both fixed and fluid, kept and lost.

1974. Tait made the tiny masterpiece, *Aerial*.

A TV aerial or the element of air? The film opens on rooftop sky and ends on a dusk sky, the end, if you like, of sky. The elements are always in some way Tait's subject.

There is even something uplifting and untouched about the lettering Tait uses to introduce her films. Here's a tiny poem of the relentlessness and beauty of the natural, all around us, I would say unnoticed, but the point of a Tait film is the noticing, the amazing colour of leaf, the sheerly beautiful thing of a dead bird looked at steadily.

Filmstrip, *Land Makar*

Filmstrip. *Place of Work*

1964. In her forties, Tait perfected the elasticity of her filmic structure with *Where I Am is Here*.

Here's a simple example of Tait syntax, the film's title, a phrase that can mean so many things. This pliant and robust multiplicity of meaning is deep in her use of the cinematic image too. The film opens with traffic sounds played against the bare branches of trees. Where are we? Tait famously added her sound after she had edited the film – and we are exactly where she would like us to open our eyes and ears, in a hold between rural and citified, past and present, part and not part (in other films she will use music, chanter and violin and voice against traffic and building work noise and silence, to re-energise this sense of place).

In what is meant to strike us as structureless, sound juxtaposes sound, image juxtaposes image, and sound and image equally meet and clash and blend in an orchestration of simple but unforced oppositions – heat and ice, personal and impersonal (a man in a room, the only personal close-up in the film, opens and closes his eyes), new and old (new pipes waiting at the back of old tenements), light and dark (moon, carlights, streetlights, Christmas lights reflecting on a black wet city street), surreal and real (the texture of road surfaces, a boot hanging like a leg in a river), timeless and fixed (a clock face with no hands, another with hands fades to black).

Meanwhile it snows on a streetcleaner, thick big snow falling all over his clean road. Anonymous people pass, looking in shops. A crocodile of schoolgirls walks up a snowy pavement – only one, at the back, turns and glances at the camera. The jaws of a sand-shifting digger open and drop sand. Ducks form an unknowing choreography. A sense of almost universal unknownness, in combination with a lack of self-consciousness, visits all these images with a sense of mystery, grace, the sudden seeing of some everyday and brilliant revelation. Steam comes off a teaspoon just used in hot tea then left on the side of a saucer, in an unbelievably beautiful shot of nothing, and everything.

Most movingly, *Where I Am is Here* is social without story. It shows people who have no idea they're being seen, living and working and doing things with a kind of quotidian care and love.

Above all it shows a kind of calm survival, a getting-on-with-it, whether in the cleaning of or traversing of a street or the putting up of a new city. It does all this by forcing nothing, by allowing images their own voice. It is meditative and calm; its seeming structurelessness is a deception; its images are reverberative, as in all working poetic structure.

Its final section is entitled *The Bravest Boat*. Images of a small boat on a calm pond, then images of a roaring fall of water. Images of all kinds of fire, then images of the city's insurance buildings and banks. Images of the waterfall, then images of lions, caged.

Where I Am is Here is a focus on the tenuousness of the journey to wherever it is we are, and the giving over of the self, first to the seeming shapelessness and meaninglessness then the unexpected shapeliness and beauty of where it is we are, and last, a suggestion that we simply give ourselves over to the astonishing and everyday richness of the experience of being here.

1964 was also the year Tait finished *Hugh MacDiarmid, A Portrait*. "I dream of poems like the breadknife that cuts three slices at once," MacDiarmid says on the soundtrack of a portrait that's a model of versatility, a meld of voice and image each illuminating the other in a way that, for all its artifice, is a new kind of nature.

Hugh MacDiarmid, the lion of Scottish poetry, the granite seriousness of the stature of the man, is what you'd expect of a portrait. Here MacDiarmid walks like a child along the kerb of an Edinburgh New Town pavement, walks along the ridge of wall outside a dour Edinburgh church. Tait films him on the very edge of things, and alively so, mischievous and unexpected, edging his way down steps towards the sea, there at the border between the different elements themselves. Never mind the detail of his house at the beginning, or the detail of MacDiarmid in the pub – unique chances in which to see him, to be witness to the live man, the usually stony-looking ridges in his hair, the deep-edged lines round his eyes. Never mind the aliveness of the poems in the voice-over, or

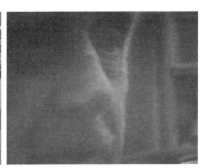

Stills, *Hugh MacDiarmid, A Portrait*

the caught aliveness of the city and the time. This is a film
that so enlivens the notion of portrait that for anyone who
sees it, MacDiarmid, the lion of Scottish poetry, giving his
surprising charming little self-shrug of a laugh at the end of
this short masterpiece, will never actually die.

1956. In her late thirties, Margaret Tait made the
masterpiece, *Rose Street*.
  "All fade away" is its opening refrain, in a girl's voice, a
Scottish song, a child singing about a mountain over the
views of a city. Rose Street was gone as soon as it was filmed
– but here it is again, 1950s Edinburgh in all its locality,
complexity, relentless traffic of merchanting and living and
playing; the light on the side of a black glass bottle on the
back of a truck, the hardened face of a man pulling a trailer,
staring right at us like a question or a challenge. The
soundtrack of Scottish drunken dirge singing, jaunty
whistling of Scottish jigs, accordion versions of Scottish songs
prompts another set of questions about Scotland itself and its
moods and natures; the voice moaning roamin in the gloamin
wi a lassie by my side ironic over the top of footage of a
masked girl-silversmith and her blowtorch in her workshop,
working. There's no forced narrative, but something which
works as both a heightened realism and a gruff poetic, and as
usual with Tait the day has a shape and that's the shape the
film takes. Who owns the street, and when? Tait's camera eye
reveals what looks random as pattern, the patterns that
people's all-day movements make on their environment.
Finally, paradoxically and craftily, the sense conveyed by this
random-seeming collage of images is of a huge revelation of
coming-together, a sense of a life communally lived.
  This is also the unexpectedly uplifting revelation of *The
Drift Back*, finished in 1956 and a rare thing for Tait – a
commissioned work, ordered and paid for by the County
Council of Orkney Education Committee, to record the return
of families to unpopulated parts of Orkney; a film with a
recognisably institutional voice-over, but a Tait film to its

core in that it won't compromise, it catches an incredible robustness and vulnerability both at once, a fragile hope in a tough landscape, and its people arrive off the boat to live in an unadulteratedly daunting and inhospitable landscape. All there is to modify this is the communal hospitable. Local men pass the whisky bottle amongst themselves, shy, embarrassed to be being filmed, but unfussily helping shift the furniture to the farm and the people into their house. The tractor slips back in the mud. It will be impossible. Then something happens which only an artist like Tait could catch and keep unsentimental. The small incomer boy rides his scooter over the wet mud and stones and through the men grouped working and sorting together: the impossible vein of playfulness in a film which educates us through mud to its end with its two small boys playing on top of what's left of an ancient Orcadian fort, top of history, top of their world.

1952. Tait was 34, and began making *Calypso* by painting in colour straight on to film stock and matching it to a soundtrack of Calypso songs.

It's like watching a heart burst open, this vibrant display of Tait's love of colour, music, rhythm, image and, most of all, open connection, as a line of colour turns from a bird into a fish into a bat into a ball into a hand. Circles become curves become people become stars become flowers become fire becomes dancers, becomes proof of the flow of things.

It's like the found heart of Tait, a viewing of this film alongside the others. It's like her imagination in essence, freed from the concrete at the same time as saturated and sated by it and all its random-seeming connections, to a point of sheer explosive happiness.

In the same year, she completed *A Portrait of Ga*, a proof of her genius for portraiture, and a film about the notion of portraiture itself and the investure of love in the seen portrait. What is film for? Why is it different from still photography, when it comes to seeing its subject? What can it tell us about someone?

How somebody moves. How somebody is still.

Still, *Calypso*

Still, *A Portrait of Ga*

Her mother sits in a landscape, keeping time to a tune with her hand. Detail is how to know someone. How she smokes. How she smiles wryly, or looks away.

A close-up of her mother's hands and the delicacy of the hands taking the wrapper off a very sticky sweet tell us everything we can know about this woman, and the care and the necessary distance, both, with which we observe those we love.

A long shot of her mother, from behind, almost running almost dancing along a rural road beneath a greyed-out rainbow is, in that miraculous Tait way, so placed, so unquaint and so natural, as to leave its viewer renewed and knowing again what it is, simply to be alive.

This is also the year in which she completed *The Lion, the Griffin and the Kangaroo*, her study of Perugia, with its opening and closing shots of stone and birds, the fixed and the moving.

All her life Tait would lovingly film people coming up and down great expanses of stone steps, because to Tait there was clearly nothing more exciting than watching the static regular line of things be brought alive and disturbed by the moving, random line. This film's theme is the learning of another language – the learning of new things, new places. It's a film that teaches itself in a new film language too: the recurrences of light and dark, of stone and air, present and past, even a combined gender voice-over, passing democratically from male to female (this in itself extraordinary, and so simple).

1951. Margaret Tait MD, 32-years old, was back from serving in the Far East with the Royal Army Medical Corps and was studying cinema under the influence of Rossellini and the neorealists in Italy at the Centro Sperimentale di Cinematografia. She formed Ancona films. She filmed her first narrative, *One is One*.

A man and a woman arrive in Rome for the day to visit the city, which neither of them knows. But almost as soon as they arrive, they lose each other. What happens? What will they do? The question is a metaphysical one: what do you do left in a strange environment by yourself?

The woman mopes momentarily. But then there's a fountain, and the surface of stone and the shapes of streets – she starts to come alive to her surroundings. The film becomes the drama of being a stranger and we interact with the woman, the stranger in the city. How do we see where we are? How do we see our surroundings? How do we see?

We watch her learn to see on her own terms. We literally watch her come alive. She moves, then literally runs, excited, from sight to sight to sight. Questions of gender, a clear subtext in *One is One*, will be a quiet preoccupation for Tait for the rest of her life. The woman looks at the statues of men. A stranger, a man, looks at her. She has to move away, look away, decorously of course, and the film becomes a further commentary on the act of looking, how and what stops us and what lets us look.

Meanwhile, *One is One* becomes more and more sensual and Buñuel-surreal. The woman hugs a pillar. She feels the grass with her bare feet. Her man friend, incidentally, the film shows us momentarily, is in a cafe smoking, in a bad mood, refusing company, by himself. But in one simple and brilliant image Tait lets us know how the woman misses the man when she unwraps two rolls for lunch and starts to eat, but puts her roll, uneaten, back on her knee in the paper wrapping beside the other roll.

But the city is seen, the place is known, the day is the opposite of wasted, instead it's freed up, discovered. *One is One* is what you might call Tait-liberated narrative, a glorious wandering, an adventure full of potential, and the whole world waiting for you to see it.

Simultaneously, of course, Tait was making the opposite of narrative. *Three Portrait Sketches*, also made in 1951, utterly refutes story, and suggests meaning lies in free association – the fall of a feather, the making of a structure out of random stones.

At the end of this film, in a final flash, the two-second-long flourish of a little bow, it's Margaret Tait herself, in her early thirties, in the Italian sun, waving goodbye.

I used to lie in wait to see the clover open
Or close,
But never saw it.
I was too impatient,
Or the movement is too subtle,
Imperceptible
And more than momentary.
— Margaret Tait, "Now", *Origins and Elements,* 1959
Margaret Tait repeatedly said she loved the notion, which she picked up from reading Lorca's lecture about Don Luis de Gongora, of 'stalking the image' when she described her own filmic practice: the equivalence of a stealthy, patient hunt. Her quite steely emphasis on open states of eye and self are something akin to the hopeless, hopeful empathy, the 'pure transcendence' that comes out of both loss and aliveness that Rilke expresses in the "9th Duino Elegy" when he says:
Perhaps we are here in order to say: house,
bridge, fountain, gate, pitcher, fruit-tree, window – ...
But to say them, you must understand,
oh to say them more intensely than the Things
themselves
ever dreamed of existing.
Tait's urge is to see so intensely that she (and we) see right through the act of seeing. John Berger, in *The Shape of a Pocket,* writes about the predicament of and the instinct for exactly this visual concentration:
it can happen, suddenly, unexpectedly, and most frequently in the half-light of glimpses, that we catch sight of another visible order which intersects with ours and has nothing to do with it. The speed of a

cinema film is 24 frames per second. God knows how many frames per second flicker past in our daily perception, but it is as if, at the brief moments I'm talking about, suddenly and disconcertingly we see between two frames. We come upon a part of the visible which wasn't destined for us ... Our customary visible order is not the only one: it co-exists with others.

This is a useful and helpful way to see Tait, as spirit-contemporary with artists like Rilke and Berger as well as a poet who, for most of her life, lived and worked against the customary visible order. She made films for no market and so, practically, allowed no market limitation. This, as she far-sightedly knew, didn't mean there was no market pressure, or no real and threatening pressure on her, as an artist working in a threatened and marginalised form, and as a woman. "You never had a chance, had you?" she writes to all the woman poets, and by inference all the women artists, in a series of poems about the domesticated and belittling roles women have been historically and mundanely meant to accept. In fact she allowed no limitation at all to the open vision and visions of her work. "For as far as I can see / There never is a conclusion," she says in one of the poems.

Malcolm Le Grice, writing about Tait and the British avant-garde film scene in *Studio International* in 1975, articulated this when he said that Tait should be considered "the only genuinely independent experimental mind in film to precede the current movement." There's no denying it. A pioneer. A modernist. A far sight. A first voice. An original. A maker. And she's nearly lost. We lose things like this all the time. She makes us, and our senses, and the world, more possible. We have to make sure we don't lose her or limit her. She refused limit; her work refuses limit.

Still. *One is One*

Still, *The Leaden Echo and the Golden Echo*

Still, *Land Makar*

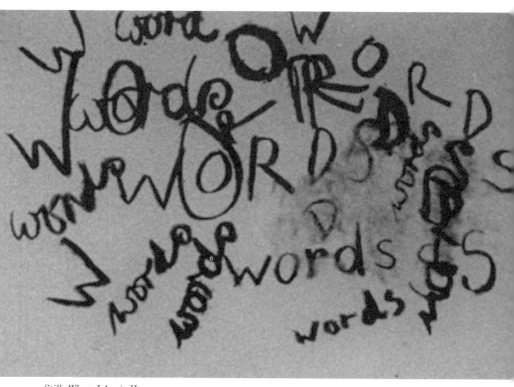

Still, *Where I Am is Here*

Where I am is here:
a patchwork for Margaret Tait

A celebration,
an argument,
some voices

Gareth Evans

For one who knows, who is closer to me than skin, who gifts me songs, who looks on the world with eyes of velvet, searching for the furthest shore of the sea ...

But sometimes
It is the time simply to say.
Just say.
But there's so much to say that by the time
    I fine it down there's only one word left
And then that word has to go too, being inadequate,
And only my eyes are left
For saying it all.
— Margaret Tait,"Ay, Ay, Ay, Dolores",
Origins and Elements, 1959

The tools. What are the tools? The tools are a glass and its wine (later a whisky close to the target); are Strauss' *Four Last Songs* and *Morgen* (its keening hope); are an evening somewhere between rain and that tomorrow; are a kind of ink and a table grained like the current.

A tool that is fully used
Gets a bloom on it
From its own essential-ness.
— Margaret Tait,
"For Using",
The Hen and the Bees, 1960

All stories begin with a place. Or rather, the telling of the
stories (is there a difference?) begins, whether spoken or not,
with this place. Once upon a time … as if the time of this
telling was first a hill from which the landscape of the story
might be viewed, and from which its topography conveyed to
the story's listeners. And from such a point, with the wind's
message and high light in mind, just as the story surrounds
the hill, so the time of the story, its moments, lie also like
fields, pastures. Its past, present and future exist for the
teller as one. They are all seen, heard and held (that is not to
say they are all known by the teller, but she knows them to be
present). This is implicitly understood by the audience, who
volunteer themselves with smiles to be led by the teller. They
are all now. In French this is *maintenant*, hand holding.

If you can see, look. If you can look, observe.
— from a book of exhortations

Without break, they walk together. The question then is: in
what order shall the story be told, what route shall be taken?

Go north. Where the light
that is we value more than
the dark that is. Where
the colour is a gift simply
because it *is*.

We launch ourselves then, from the table. From the table, the pen, the paper like an island in the grain. There is a sense, hesitant, reaching, like the hand of a baby as it finds it can hold, that her films might be taken

Still, *The Big Sheep*

as landscape, not just for what they catch, but in themselves, as a topography, marine because fluid, joining. There is, somewhere, just behind seeing, the intimation that place can help us. Place in its dance. Geographies of light. And how the movements inside them can reveal the project.

The films, then, are as maps and the goal of maps. The films as archipelago. Just as we, ourselves alone, are still part of the throng. Concentrations made greater in the assembly. Still singular selves, but joined beneath the waves.

Indeed, this text might be, to borrow, "a black and white film of a black-like street full of its own sort of colour ..." where the hues come from all the people walking / talking. So, as the walk / talk along Rose Street becomes a threaded narrative of engaged diversion, and people become their golden bar-room shadows, like stained glass in motion, so we raise a glass together and feed in our penny or so.

There is a different mind for islands. Tait had such a mind. Wilful as an outcrop. Self-defining. Clearly in the ocean, she sought local detailing. The etched trajectory, the fecund spill. Things verdantly over-lapping. She was the light-teller of daily tales, hers a borderless philosophy: reading all the scripts, from signage grabs to nature's text, from boats, leaves, houses, street, to soil, rock, traceries of war. Working on the interstitial, intertitled, overlooked, what other response can there be than the wonderful "Aha!"

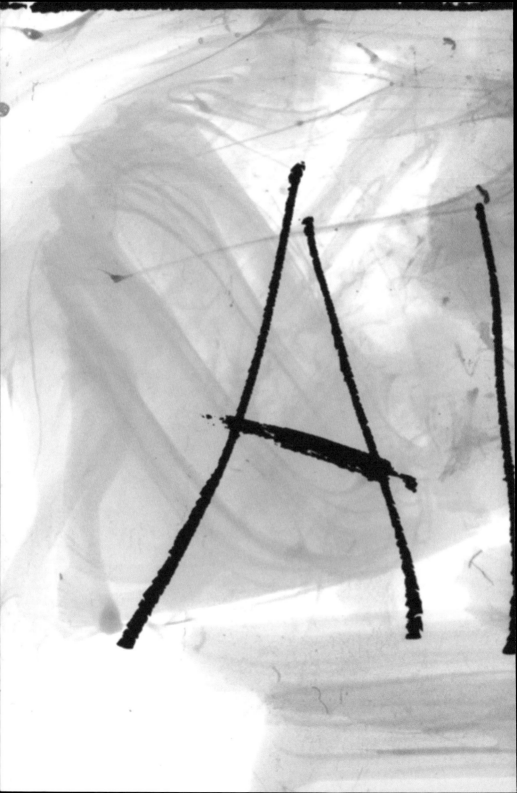

I have picked up a few curious things from the shore of the
great ocean of time.
— George Mackay Brown, *Beside the Ocean of Time,* 1994

Her eye's magpie retrieval, keeping all, in time. Look again
and deeper. Only connect.

The undressed back of buildings. 'Keep Clear' – she
ignored that.

No ideas but in things.
— William Carlos Williams, *Paterson,* 1963

It is utterly beyond our power to measure the change
of things by time. Quite the contrary, time is an
abstraction, at which we arrive by the change of things.
— Ernst Mach, *The Science of Mechanics,* 1883

A clock face in mist. A clock without hands. Neither stopped
nor pushing on. But a totality called now. A deeper time than
clocks.

Thought gathers, like a shock of gulls over the night boat's
return through the sound. White as ash in the turning air.
The harbour gleams, jewels on a bed of velvet. Yearning.

Desire fuels her. It carries her past … no money, past the
sometime isolation, past belief's ebb and flow. She runs on the
application of pure will.

Every individual does penance for separation from
the boundless.
— Anaximander, *On Nature,* sixth-century

An imperfect poem goes on seeking the silence …
After the perfect poem – which no poet will write –
the second-best poem is silence …
image, contrast, symbol …
— George Mackay Brown

... that contact
with the world
in which
(for which)
I live ...
voices, steps
little gusts, plants, things
we love in balance.
— Richard Caddel, *Uncertain Time*, 1990

We say, Ah, but a life is short: a shout, a kiss, a bell.
— Jim Lewis, *The King is Dead*, 2003

What does a person need – really need? A few pounds
of food each day, heat and shelter, six feet to lie down
in – and some form of working activity that will yield
a sense of accomplishment.
— Sterling Hayden, *Wanderer*, 1963

She thought she saw a model for herself in the
order and simplicity of the sparrow's call.
— Robert Stone, *Outerbridge Reach*, 1992

The earth to stand on and to eat,
The water to drink and to wash with,
The air to breathe and to move through,
The fire to warm us
    And to light us,
    To take us into the beyond,
    Into the world of the imagination...
— Margaret Tait, "Four or Ninety or ∞ Or What",
Origins and Elements, 1959

There is an evolutionary question around the development of
the eye. Its myriad components redundant without all the
others, serving no other prior purpose. But all developing
ready for assemblage.

And then it is.

This afternoon I took a long walk because I felt I needed it, first around the cathedral, then past the new church, and then along the dyke, where the mills are that one sees in the distance as one walks near the station. There is so much expressed in this familiar landscape and surrounding; it seems to say: "Be of good courage; fear not."
— Vincent van Gogh, letter from Dordrecht, 1877

Let the beauty that we love be that which we do. For there are hundreds of ways to kneel and kiss the ground.
— Rumi, twelfth-century

The thing about poetry is you have to keep doing it.
People have to keep making it.
The old stuff is no use
Once it's old.
— Margaret Tait, "Now", *Origins and Elements*, 1959

The girl who kicks a little stone then looks to jump to its new position. Then again, again. Is this not the process of making in one?

Work as if you were in the early days of a better nation.
— Alasdair Gray

When we get our spiritual house in order, we'll be dead. This goes on. You arrive at enough certainty to be able to make your way, but it is making it in darkness. Don't expect faith to clear things up for you. It is trust, not certainty.
— Flannery O'Connor, letter to Louise Abbot, 1959

Still, Where I Am is Here

The grief for all the world which grips my heart
Un-nerves me and makes nonsense of the glee
With which I'd greet the Spring.
— Margaret Tait, "Sprung Sonnet", *Origins and Elements,* 1959

The world has no pity on a man who cannot do or
produce something it thinks worth money.
— George Gissing, *New Grub Street,* 1891

No locks.
No bolts, bars nor keys.
— Margaret Tait, "Locklessness", *The Hen and the Bees,* 1960

Live your life so that the fear of death can never enter your
heart. When you arise in the morning, give thanks for the
morning light. Give thanks for your life and strength. Give
thanks for your food and for the joy of living. And if perchance
you see no reason for giving thanks, rest assured the fault is in
yourself. — Ascribed to Chief Tecumseh

Once upon a time, there was a big storm at night in the city of
spas, and the little boy got up into this teeming dark,
stumbled into his parent's room and said, "Mummy,
the moon is banging."

I'm out here now
On the roof. Look!
I had to get nearer the sky,
For the city was too full of rooms
And I can't be content with a window.

It's too small a thing to accept the ready-made frame.
We builders must keep making our own cities.
Oh, please
Don't fell the trees
For your city, because I need them for mine.
— Margaret Tait, "But Why Not Try this Method",
Subjects and Sequences, 1960

Where are we?
  Here.
      Islands in the stream. That is what and where we are.
      Where is she?
      Dweller on the threshold ...

  Don't be frightened.
  Look Out!
  Meet in the open, and take courage
  — Margaret Tait, "Attack", *The Hen and the Bees,* 1959

Where I Am is Here

The unassailable work. The ur-piece. From its overture in
tree branch, mind-leaping off into sky and light, conceived as
music in seven movements, with the constant refrains of a
life's daily round, this is the hearth of the oeuvre entire.

Refrains again and again to get closer. Polishing the grain
of things to reveal them.

Where the writing hand soon realises that word is
redundant, that it writes itself to cancellation. Get closer. And
looking becomes an argument for biography, for the collective
project, for existence. How every image layers its meaning
with another through the seeming randomness, but really
body- or blood-directed elision of experience with film. From
building site to beach at dusk is this life (*Complex*). It is made
and washed away (*Now and Gone*), like steam on a teaspoon.
Houses, vases, cameras, toys, moment, weather, that rose
light of late afternoon – all of them *The Bravest Boat*, drifting
on their own trembling shadow.

But in the hours between, children will mark their
passage on to the page of the slope. The joy of looking and
looking again. Learning through repetition. The instinctual
poetry of childhood, the reading of the world in ways that
make a bodily sense. And slowly the world survives each day.

It endures beyond our direct sensual experience of it, our seeing. It ripples out like tree rings into time as the kernel of knowing grows.

While she leaps with light from the window out (*Here and Now*) and everywhere, which is close by, because it all comes back to the way a street is crossed and re-crossed. How a snail navigates the paving after rain. How a child raises its own head.

And how she allows everything its own claim, its gathering moment (in close or mid shot; the world is already established, it does not need setting up) but how she refuses separation. There is no 'backstory'. Nothing is relegated. 'Come and see this.'

The democracy of her looking that becomes a unity. There is only one thing, and that is all things. Film and gardens tell us this. A growing world, a green weave. Ceaseless motion and change. Rising and dispersal. So, how she enables the jaws of a mechanical digger, as agents of both collapse but also a melancholy enduring. Like some heavy slow animals making their unique way across the centuries.

Snow, when it comes, is the perennial *tabula rasa*. When the eye can rest a beat. The fresh page, latent with becoming (and we script our walking as a small line of its winter poem). She finds it falling through the single unobscured pane.

As he looked, the sky mysteriously darkened and chilled. From far off came the mutter of the unsatisfied thunder, and he knew it was the signal of the snow rolling over the sea. He turned, and felt its breath on him.
— D.H. Lawrence, *The Man Who Loved Islands*, 1927

And light over all of it like the single sheet of early lovers. Inside each other. We don't stop at our skin.

But the thresholds make us one. Shore, kerb (remember Hugh MacDiarmid tightroping it), window, door. Eyes. From head to world, in to out, house to street, bar, park, field, earth. Us on earth like few film makers show.

Still, *Where I Am is Here*

Still, *Where I Am is Here*

From being alone to all.

This shaping of space for living. For our various selves to
find their room. Threshing the world for image. Trawling.
Her art a golden echo of the world's being. Pantheisms of
the island edge.

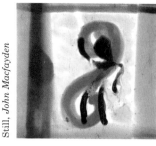

Still, *John Macfayden*

And colour often as its outrider;
her joyous immersion in it
and where it lives. Her calypso,
taking a line for a dance. All the
work animation really; things
become other things;
metamorphosis. The green fuse
firing through it all, like Orquil
Burn ("running water is a useful
force"). Like bird song, child song, the carrying songs of
children playing, like pigeons in gather and shift; the street's
dawn, day and dusk chorus, the vulnerable sounds of being.

Like Lilane's lament for *Hilltop Pibroch*; the sound of the
Earth's sorrow.

Then how, in a single sequence, of seconds only, she
establishes the entire course of human agency on earth.

The fire flickers / An apple, pen and ink on the universal
table / A bite of the fruit by an unseen mouth / The fire
flickers / An apple, pen and ink on the universal table / A
hand picks the apple, makes the bite we saw. Winding
Promethean gifts in with the Edenic tasting of awareness,
and cutting both with the tools of imaginative response, she
makes one of the clearest statements in cinema on the
emergence of consciousness. Indeed, the cuts work as
perceptual jolts into that awareness.

Then again, with ambiguous fire, erasing and cleansing,
as its axle, she cuts a statement on value and being that is
both politically potent and metaphysically active. Cuts from
signage of banks and insurers to children piling a street
bonfire. This is her art, this rippling concision of moment, of
implied reach.

The miraculous is not extraordinary but the common mode
of existence. It is our daily bread. Whoever really
has considered the lilies of the field or the birds of the
air and pondered the improbability of their existence in
this warm world within the cold and empty stellar
distances will hardly balk at the turning of water into
wine – which was, after all, a very small miracle. We
forget the greater and still continuing miracle by which
water (with soil and sunlight) is turned into grapes.
— Wendell Berry, "Christianity and the Survival of
Creation", *Sex, Economy, Freedom and Community*, 1993

There's a whole country at the foot of the stone
If you care to look.
— Margaret Tait, "The Scale of Things",
The Hen and the Bees, 1959

We are part of the whole which we call the universe,
but it is an optical delusion of our mind that we think
we are separate. This separateness is like a prison for
us. Our job is to widen the circle of compassion so we
feel connected to all people and all situations.
— Albert Einstein, *New York Post*, 28 November 1972

Yonder. – What high as that! We follow, now we follow. –
        Yonder, yes yonder, yonder,
Yonder.
— Gerard Manley Hopkins, "The Leaden Echo and the
Golden Echo", 1882

Blue.
    Black.
        Permanent.

Memory is a present which never stops going past.
— Octavio Paz

She shows us that the work of such a moment lasts a lifetime.
She asks us to ask ourselves the reason for our days. She asks
us why and then she shows us how.

Stop, look, listen. Live.

And tomorrow the sun will shine again,
And on the path that I shall take
it will unite us, lucky ones, again
Amid this sun-breathing earth.

And to the beach, broad and blue-waved,

we shall climb down, quiet and slow.
Speechless we shall gaze in each other's eyes,
And the speechless silence of happiness will
        fall on us.
— Richard Strauss, *Morgen,* 1894

He will cover you with his plumage and under his wing
then you will rest. — W.G. Sebald, *Unrecounted,* 2004

No little pain in leaving world behind. But has it not been
(fin) fine?

All things shining.
— Terence Malick, *The Thin Red Line*
                                                    – That's all Folks! –
yes I am lying in the ground
but my lips are moving.
— Osip Mandelstam

                                                    End ...

Stills, *Where I Am is Here*

Still, *Where I Am is Here*

Still, *Where I Am is Here*

Still, *Aerial*

Margaret Tait: marks of time

Lucy Reynolds

There is a short sequence in Margaret Tait's film *Where I Am is Here* in which an apple, a pen and an inkpot make up a quiet still life on a tabletop. Suddenly and unexpectedly a bite mark appears in the apple. In this animated second there is no trace of the perpetrator, just teethmarks in the flesh of the fruit. The rest of the still life remains undisturbed – a shot of slowly dying flames in a grate and then Tait returns us to the still life. Now the apple is whole again, a hand reaches for it, picks it out of the still life and into the dark space off-camera. A second later the same hand returns the apple to its position in the still life, with the bite-mark first made in that animated moment now returned.

This playful sequence, just a few moments in a much longer film, goes to the heart of what Margaret Tait achieves in her extraordinary body of films. Tait's moment of animation has the quality of simple magic, a conjuring trick. Unexpectedly, it disrupts the flow of time and reverses it. It is as if Tait is revelling in the ability of the filmmaking process to play with our perceptions of cinematic time and space, revealing the gaps. Her sleight of hand is achieved by

elegantly simple means, changing the temporal order of a sequence of images. Like other experimental film makers, Tait explored how formal processes such as editing could transform images and their meaning. Her delicate trickery can be traced in the films of Gunvor Nelson, Joyce Weiland or even the spatial discontinuities of Maya Deren's *Meshes of the Afternoon*, or *At Land*. However, Tait's interest in how film time functions does not only surface in the formal experimentation of this animated still life. It could be argued that she evokes a notion of time more profoundly in the way she frames natural beauty, and documents the changing spaces and landscapes around her, imbuing her images with an almost metaphysical significance.

In this regard, Tait's apple, pen and inkpot could be considered akin to the Vanitas paintings of seventeenth-century Holland. Their still lives of fruit and flowers always included a visual clue, as emphatic as a skull, or as subtle as a fly, to remind the viewer that the plentiful life portrayed on the canvas would pass and turn to dust. The bite in Tait's apple fulfils the same function as the painted skull, marking the passage of time. It denotes the future fate of the apple, to be eaten and decay. This metaphysical notion of time recurs throughout Tait's films, not only in her still lives of everyday objects, but in her framing of nature, the landscapes of her native Orkney and the streets of Edinburgh. Tait's films are filled with images of natural beauty, often of places and things overlooked, commonplace or close to the ground: the lichen on the stones of a bridge by Orquil Burn, for example, or blowing tree leaves in *Aerial*. All of these images allude to the different temporal states of the natural world. The lichen signifies the aged quality of the bridge, whilst the leaves in *Aerial* will soon blow away. The question of how far Tait intended these allusions is clearly felt in her subtle interventions into the order of things. It is found in her quiet, but insistent, presence outside the frame, in the commentary of her voice-over or in the significance of the patterns and rhythms in her editing, based on the forms of poetry.

Orkney

The islands of Orkney were the subject of many of Margaret Tait's films, and remained a central theme throughout her life. She was born and grew up there and her images are shaped by this profound personal attachment. Tait's Orkney is a psycho-geographical landscape which maps the people and places by her intimate experience of them. The historian Simon Schama has described the notion of landscape as "a tradition built from a rich deposit of myths, memories, and obsessions", (*Landscape and Memory*, 1996). If this is the case then Tait's films are a form of excavation. The intense focus of her camera on the surfaces and contours of the land itself uncovers not only the contemplative natural beauty in its details, but a sense of the histories embedded there. There are the remains of the old army camp, for example, or the dried up lake once used by the farm. Like rings in a tree trunk, her gentle images trace circles of time, from the wider implications of political and economical changes that affect the island to personal memories and experiences, and those of the islanders. Often these images are reinforced and counter-pointed by a rich mix of sound, from the ambient notes in nature, to Tait's own quiet commentary and the music of the islanders, notably the Orkney Strathspey and Reel Society.

In Tait's images of Orkney the land is portrayed neither as a backdrop to human agency, as in narrative cinema, nor as the remote and uninhabited spaces of Michael Snow's film *La Region Centrale* (1971), or Chris Welsby's *Welsh Mountain in Seven Days* (1974). Tait's Orkney is an active space, in which the people who inhabit it are embedded, working the land and using its resources. Tait's films are as much portraits of an equal balance between the natural environment and those who live from it as they are images of natural beauty. Rather than describe the landscape in the lateral arc of a panning camera, as a conventional cinematographer might, Tait's vision is composed of many small parts. Her camera concentrates on details in the landscape: stones, grass, water, signs of human presence like a derelict boat or the distant chimney top. Her scale is human, less an attempt to encompass the breadth of the landscape as to focus on its many surfaces and textures. This is particularly true of her 1955 film *Orquil Burn*, in which she films her journey along the banks of a burn that runs across the island. Tait walks the path of the burn, starting where it enters the sea and following it up to its origin in the wet Orkney hills. The linear path of the stream literally creates the linear narrative of Tait's tale and alludes to the personal timelines connected to the burn, composed of the collective histories of the Orcadians as well as her own. She introduces the viewer to the characters along its route with a direct address: "This is Uncle Peter and elderly Spot." They are intimate portraits, again reminding us of the close ties Tait has to this land, evoking and describing the space of the landscape through her naming; ("the old army camp," "the place in the burn the children call 'the deep part'.") Tait reminds us that the burn's weaving course is a meeting place between the different rhythms of time in Orkney's natural world and its people; from the deeper echo of history and memory to the temporal shifts of passing clouds and the children's reed boats carried down stream.

In *A Portrait of Ga*, personal and Orcadian histories intertwine in a moving film portrait of Tait's own mother. "It's the grandchildren who call her Ga, and I suppose I called her mother Ga, but I only dimly remember that grandmother, my mother's mother." This is the passage of time mapped through bloodlines and generations. It conjures a landscape of Orkney filtered through the memories of family histories and personal recollection, Tait's dimly remembered grandmother, for example. The sprightly elderly woman that is Ga is caught in snatches and glances, by Tait's camera.

In conventional cinematic portrayals of landscape human figures occupy the prominent position in relation to the land, forming what P. Adams Sitney has referred to as "the hierarchical distinction between human action and natural setting", ("Landscape in the cinema: the rhythms of the world and the camera", *Landscape, Natural Beauty and the Arts*, 1993). By contrast, the heightened sense of texture and pattern created in Tait's close-ups makes Ga seem almost to meld with the patterns of nature. In one particular sequence the warm hues of her tartan coat have the same density of colour as the heather behind her.

However, Ga is an active element of that landscape, constantly in motion throughout the film: smoking, talking, digging, walking away from the camera towards the loch with some purpose. Depicted in the dim interior of her croft, the camera focuses a fleeting poignant moment on her still moving hands, liver-spotted with age, as she struggles to remove a sweet from its translucent wrapper. There is a startling clarity in the way that Tait's camera captures details such as these. A clear-eyed distance which lifts the image above the saccharine or the mawkish. Like the sequence with the apple in *Where I Am is Here* it shows Tait's ability to produce quiet images of rare beauty, which still manage to disrupt the expectation of the viewer.

Ghosts

The unique quality of Tait's images, their ability to combine an intensely personal perspective with a sense of distance, may have been shaped by an early period of study at the Centro Sperimentale di Cinematografia film school in Rome. Here she absorbed the ideas of neorealism and a commitment to the documentary film form that infuses her work. The subjective detail of her images was sharpened and counterbalanced by the documentary rigour she gained as a student. Rather than beauty for its own sake, her films demonstrate the need to develop a film language that could portray the people and landscapes close to her with a kind of truth. "I'm looking for what's there, seeing things as they are." At first her images look almost simple, modest perhaps: children playing in a street, or flowers in a garden. However, as *Orquil Burn* has shown, a closer viewing reveals these fleeting moments as part of a complex montage of imagery, a

Stills, *A Portrait of Ga*

web of associations woven against an equally complex pattern of ambient sound, indigenous music and spoken word. As in the cinema of the neorealists, the performers in her films are non-professionals: friends, family, passers-by. They are sometimes unaware of the camera and sometimes asked, as in *A Portrait of Ga* to be the subject of its scrutiny. The textures of the ordinary lives that Tait explores in her films are underpinned with a keen political sensibility. She records and monitors the changes in the streets of Edinburgh and in the landscapes of Orkney, weighing the balance of the old traditional ways: of farming and keeping shop, against the changing times. There is a note of censure against the political changes imposed on the land from distant parliaments and businesses although, unlike a more conventional documentary maker, her films are devoid of didacticism. Their purpose is not so much to educate as to keep record of the people and places within her immediate orbit.

In *On the Mountain*, as with so many of her films, Tait's documentary clarity merges with experimental form. A testament to the changes on an Edinburgh street where she had her film company, Ancona Films, for over twenty years, this was about 'the life of the street'. While films like *Orquil Burn* trace changing time in the contours of the land, here she places images from two different time frames next to each other in literal contrast. *On the Mountain* is a film record of Rose Street made in 1973 with an earlier film of the same street enclosed within it, credits and leader intact. Tait made the first Rose Street film in 1956 and, played against the more prosaic colour images of Rose Street's 1970s incarnation, its black and white images have an exotic nostalgia. Like a pressed leaf that falls unexpectedly from the pages of a book, it releases with a jolt the sensations and atmospheres of a former time. Where are those people now? The girls silhouetted in the low sun playing hopscotch, the Teddy Boys kicking a ball. They are summoned back as their former selves to mark the passage of time, not only in its changes but also in its sense of continuity, of remaining the same. For Tait's camera finds the same window cleaner washing the same shop windows in 1973, only now the shop has changed its name. This implies a disjunction between the temporal and spatial dimensions of the film image, creating a looking glass world in which Rose Street and the window cleaner occupy the same space simultaneously but in different time frames, 1956 and 1973. Two Rose Streets co-exist, reflecting back on to each other their shared but dissimilar spaces. The viewer follows the discontinuities between them, now actively implicated in Tait's game of memory as they read the signs of change across two time frames.

In the simple illusion of an apple bitten twice Tait was the conjurer; in *On the Mountain* she allows film's fundamental ability to record and hold moments of time to conjure its own ghosts back to life. The filmstrip's inert material is reactivated to release the spectral sounds and images of a long-past Edinburgh. By including the leaders and credits, referents to the materiality of film itself rather than its images, it seems that Tait understands the tangible power of the moving image to resuscitate time. If her images of Orkney show time as an implicit substance, traces in the landscape, here they are presented to the viewer directly, as a document of changing space. Each incarnation of Rose Street haunts the other, neither being discernible as the definitive past or present representation of the street. Tait makes an explicit reference to the ghosts in her film, focusing her camera on a discarded handbill lying on the cobbles which has the word Ghosts as its title. She needn't have laboured this point, for the spectral presences of *On the Mountain* are invoked in the patina of the film material itself and the co-existent Rose Streets which brush against each other in her film.

The Leaden Echo and the Golden Echo

The relationship between the word and the image is an intrinsic aspect of Tait's filmmaking, sometimes taking the form of a voice-over, caught in the notes of a song and often

Still, *Rose Street*

Still, *On the Mountain*

directed through the lyrical forms of poetry. In *Orquil Burn*, for example, the interpretative phrases of Tait's quiet commentary feel almost like haiku in their sparse clearness. Though akin to the explanatory device of the voice-over, Tait's marrying of word and image has a personal insistence, which ultimately foils that sense of documentary distance. As a poet herself, Tait's own verse is often woven into her films, the rhythm and density of the poetic form providing its subject matter and structure. Tait explored the experimental application of poetry to film structure throughout her career, seeing the making of 'film poems' as her 'life's work'. This is notable in *Colour Poems* and *Where I Am is Here*, which are divided into a number of short films, like the stanzas or verses of a poem. Preceded by a title, each sequence contains its own logic and tempo, yet contributes to the overall shape and flow of the film. Tait breaks down the momentum of linear narrative so that these passages can be read as discrete and contemplative pools of time in the wider temporal flow of the film.

In *The Leaden Echo and the Golden Echo* Tait specifically "matches images of my own" to Gerard Manley Hopkins' poem of the same name, transforming the poet's words through the personal prism of her image-making process. Tait's films share the same poetic structures and intimate perspective of another pioneering woman film maker, Marie Menken, and like Menken, Tait often gathered her images by a process of accumulation, filming intermittent moments and events observed over protracted periods of time. The lyrical images for Menken's 1962 film *Notebook* were amassed over a twenty-year period, and the images for *The Leaden Echo and the Golden Echo* were also gathered in this gradual way, "started in 1948, set aside and returned to now and again, and completed in 1955". As with much of Tait's work, the images in the film have this sense of domestic and familiar detail, filtering Hopkins' poem through the people and landscapes close to her. The images hover between informal set-ups and tableaux and a keen-eyed recording of objects and events caught in passing. The associative linkage of word to image shares the almost hallucinatory detail evoked in the poem, an acute focus on the rippled surface of a stream, for instance, playing against "the wimpled-water-dimpled, not-by-morning-matched face". The alliterative rhyming, carried through Hopkins' words, finds a visual equivalent in the associative sequences of Tait's montage; an image of towering pine trees is followed by a church interior as she conjures their shared sense of hush and height. Threads of association such as this weave intricate lateral and linear patterns between Hopkins' rhythms and Tait's pictures, held in place by her consummate editing skills.

Hopkins' poem was a fitting choice for Tait. Like a Vanitas still life, it is permeated by an awareness of the fragility and balance of life and death in nature, its darker notes resonate against the images of beauty in Tait's film, arresting any sense of reverie in the viewer. Like the Metaphysical poets John Donne and Andrew Marvell, intrinsic to Hopkins' celebration of the beauty of nature is a lament for its passing: "is there none such, nowhere known some, bow or brooch or braid or brace, lace, latch or catch or key to keep / Back beauty, keep it, beauty, beauty, beauty, ... from vanishing away?" In *The Leaden Echo and the Golden Echo*, as in all her films, Tait has an answer for Hopkins' question. Using the medium's ability to arrest and replay time, she offers "a key to keep back beauty", catching it in the clear small moments of her mother's hands, an Orkney stream or children playing in an Edinburgh street. True to her documentary roots, she fashions these marks of time from the matter of everyday encounter, subtle but significant moments. They resonate in the Orkney flower dipping to the wind and in the experimental twist of a twice-bitten apple.

Still, *The Leaden Echo and the Golden Echo*

Still, Orquil Burn

Still, *Place of Work*

In her own words

Margaret Tait was interviewed twice for television, once by
James Wilson with director Keith Alexander for BBC
Scotland's *Spectrum* series (transmitted 5 January 1979), and
once by Tamara Krikorian with director Margaret Williams
for Channel Four, as part of a series of profiles jointly funded
with the Arts Council (transmitted 25 April 1983). She was
dissatisfied with both. Both were shot on film and necessarily
focused on getting succinct statements about the films she
had agreed might be extracted in the programme. Neither
allowed the sustained conversation she would have preferred.
But given the scarcity of her own writings on her work, these
interviews offer a rare opportunity to 'hear her voice'. The
following extracts have been augmented by material filmed
but not used in the programmes, a sound-only recording by
Wilson and Alexander, and an additional 'imagined' section of
interview Tait wrote halfway through the filming, to suggest a
line of questioning for Krikorian. The transcripts are held in
the AHRB British Artists' Film and Video Study Collection
at Central Saint Martins, University of the Arts, London,
and are used with the interviewers' permission.

Film School and Saint Francis

I did medicine first – graduated here in Edinburgh in 1941, when I was 23. Later in the War, I served in the East, in the Royal Army Medical Corps until 1946 when I was de-mobbed. I began writing screenplays – for features, that is, story films – while still practising medicine, but hadn't had any taken. I'd gone to Italy in the spring of 1950, to stay in Perugia and do some research (I thought) on Saint Francis of Assisi, because I felt he'd be a good subject for a film. I intended writing a screenplay, based on the Saint Francis story, and selling it, or trying to sell it. It was while I was there, in Italy, that summer, that I heard about the Rome [Film] School, and I heard too of course that [Roberto] Rossellini was already doing a film about Saint Francis – *Francesco, Giullare di Dio* (1950). So that was that. Anyway, I had had no success in getting screenplays taken. I thought that the writing / directing course at the Rome school would aid me in knowing how to construct a screenplay. I had learned enough Italian in Perugia to make studying in Rome possible, so I started on a two-year course at the Centro Sperimentale di Cinematografia in the autumn of 1950. I paid for it out of what was left of my army gratuity, and earnings. I could live quite frugally in Italy, without any hardship. And I coached some pupils in English. (to TK)

Three Portrait Sketches and 'treating everything equally'

In one of the early portrait films I made in Rome – I did three short portraits – one of the participants said of the filming of one of the others, that, "yes, that's what I like, everything treated equally – the woman standing there, and the leaf on the wall, it's all got equal significance." Well, I don't think I thought I was doing that. I thought I was filming the woman, you see. But it must be inherent in me that I treat the other things in the frame as being just as important. And I suppose that this is perhaps related to the way a painter would treat the different things on the canvas or a piece of paper – that he's put them all there. I mean you know you put them there and it's not by accident. (to JW)

Still, *Three Portrait Sketches*

Hugh MacDiarmid

So you used the structure of MacDiarmid's poem to pace the film?

Well, you see, this poem that I used, it's called "Somersault" and the lines:

> I lo'e the stishie
> O' Earth in space
> Breengin' by
> At a haliket pace.

suggested to me the poet as a circus performer really enjoying balancing on the high wire, or very thin line.

> A wecht o' hills
> Gangs wallopin' owre,
> Sine a whummlin' sea
> Wi' a gallus glower.

And I asked Christopher [Hugh MacDiarmid was the pseudonym of Christopher Murray Grieve] if he thought he could walk along as if he was balancing the Earth, making the Earth turn round with his own foot, and he thought he could do that, and so this is what he is doing.

> The West whuds doon
> Like the pigs at Gadara,
> But the East's aye there
> Like a sow at the farrow.

And he walks east, throws his notebook into the waste paper basket; and that's what I used that poem for, with his permission ... I was only trying to show one or two aspects of him – my view of him. I didn't know him all that well, to make a penetrating portrait of the man, and I was approaching it from the point of view of what I had read of his, really. (to TK)

Where I Am is Here

Where I Am is Here seems to me to be one of the first films where your own poetic style comes to the fore.
Yes, well, that's understandable, because there had really been quite a long interval since I last made a film. I had been writing, writing poetry. After I finished *Rose Street* I did attempt to get [*Rose Street*] taken for cinema or TV – I think I have a letter signed by Lew Grade (politely) declining – it didn't seem possible to sell short films, really, so I had to stop making films of that kind. But in 1963 I started *Where I Am is Here*, before the MacDiarmid portrait, although they overlap really in time. By that time I just felt I wanted to make a film, but there was absolutely no point in making it specifically for a market, say, when there wasn't a market, and that the only point at all in making a film with your own time, your own equipment – just making one in that way – was to do it on the level of poetry, and to be as absolutely serious about making the thing as well as you possibly could. And who said that "the art of cinema is the art of composing in images"? Images and sound are equally important. One thinks of sound in terms of duration; I think you can only think of sound in terms of duration, whereas you don't necessarily naturally think of an image in terms of duration. (to TK)

I'm more interested in filming the landscape, even if it's a minute landscape, than in shooting the scenery. And here again we come back to Scotland, bonnie Scotland, where I think there is this great temptation when people get out with their cameras to shoot the scenery, because it's there and it's marvellous, and you haven't seen that particular view before, so let's get a shot of that, and it's very nice from over here, and so on ... So *Where I Am is Here* was minutely examining the landscape of Edinburgh, or the townscape. (to JW)

The Big Sheep

The Big Sheep, although it seems in a way a different kind of film, has the same sort of repetitive structure ... the tourist buses coming north match the sheep transporters going south, and then the lambs running down among the pens at the lamb sale, to my mind anyway, match the burn running down over the rocks at the end of the film ... The full title of the film is *Cora Mor – The Big Sheep*. And Cora Mor was the nickname the Highlanders gave to the Cheviot sheep which replaced people in the glens at the time of the 'improvements', what, almost 200 years ago – and those memories of the Clearances are still very alive in the Highlands. And I wanted to make a picture of a place where people still remembered those things, or they remembered them through their parents and grandparents. But the memories are still there. (to TK)

There's no commentary in *The Big Sheep* apart from a local man quoting the Highlander of two centuries ago saying: "why don't you get your sheep to go and fight for you?" I don't think it's about the Clearances exactly. You can't live there without some sort of allusion to the Clearances because there's a feeling of them all around you ... But if it's about anything it is about the place as it is now. (to JW)

Still, *The Big Sheep*

82

Colour Poems

I had painted on film a bit, before, in sort of dance films,
[*Painted Eightsome,* 1970] but in *Colour Poems* I was trying
to do it rather differently. Instead of the usual kind of
animation, I was doing the opposite, in a sense. I was trying
to keep the picture as still as possible, and get the opposite
effect, you know, of Duchamp's *Nude Descending a Staircase,*
where you see several phases in one picture. I was trying to
keep my picture still, over a number of frames, but just
allowing for the natural shiver that there's bound to be; and
this was to illustrate a slightly shaky memory I had, of what
of course in World terms was a very significant time in this
century, the time of the Spanish Civil War. But my memories
of it were simply of newspaper reports and of some people
who had gone away to it and had come back, and I couldn't
quite take it all in at all, really. So, between Sorley MacLean's
poem about not having gone to the Spanish Civil War, and
something of Lorca – I got the title from this book: *El Numen
de las Ramas,* [from "Vals en las Ramas" in *Poet in New York,*
1940] which I translated as *Numen of the Boughs.* (I don't
know if it is a correct translation.) I had started a poem in
words, and I tried to complete it on film; that was what I
was doing. (to TK)

Still, *Colour Poems*

83

Aerial

Aerial – maybe does seem a difficult film, in a way, but *Aerial* is really very simple if you allow yourself to respond to it instead of trying to follow it intellectually. There's no narrative and no argument; the theme's more like a musical theme, conjured out of the whole rather than presented as points to be taken. There's a general theme of the four elements: earth, air, fire and water, and only in a different order, air, water, earth, fire and then air again ... but just [presented] as a sort of song, or even a nursery rhyme. I don't understand musical structure. I cannot really follow the structure of a piece of music when I am listening to it, but from what's said about musical structure I do see a resemblance in the way I construct those films. (to TK)

Still, *Aerial*

Place of Work and Tailpiece

In more recent years, I've been working in Orkney. I had to give up the Rose Street premises in 1973, but we had effectively moved North even before then. *The Big Sheep* was made in Sutherland but edited at Rose Street, and *Aerial* and *Colour Poems* were made on Orkney and edited there, although not in any sense about Orkney. Then in 1975–76 I made two films, *Place of Work* and *Tailpiece* – *Tailpiece* being a coda to *Place of Work* – very much lodged in a place, using a house and garden, which you might think of more as a subject for painting than for film ... (to TK)

The house is called Buttquoy and is in Kirkwall. I was really trying to paint (as it were) this self-contained place – a house and garden, in among streets, with glimpses of the town and of the sea and islands from the windows – because I knew it so well, rather than tell any story about its having been the family home and so on. That, in fact, as a fact, doesn't show in the film except in the sense that because it was that, I could approach some of its secrets with confidence. By 'secrets' I mean just things like – which doors lead to where, how far the light reaches in, the feeling of being on the stairs and all sorts of other things which I have carried about with me without necessarily thinking about them, but which led me, eventually, to point the camera at one thing rather than another. And since I had helped to make the garden, and in the seven years up to the film had been working in it quite a lot, mostly by myself, I knew my way around those slopes and planes and bits of courtyard. So that's why you probably do get a feeling of 'presence' in that film – my presence, there with the camera – perhaps the presence of other people who had been there before, and even your own presence in the picture, as you look at it.

    Place of Work is in colour, and the sounds are, ostensibly, happening in the scene. My voice, on the phone, voices of

passers-by and of children playing nearby, sounds of
road-works digging into the same red clay that the garden
originally consisted of, the pop music supposed to be being
played by the painters working on the windows, me speaking
to the postman. In *Tailpiece*, which is in black and white, the
sound is much more clearly and recognizably an added track.
Sounds drift through the house (as it were) which are allusive
in nature; the allusions don't have to be caught, as such, so
long as it comes through that they relate to presences in the
house. To be explicit, some are to do with other work of my
own, films I have worked on in the house, work I have done
elsewhere, like the translations from the book lying on the
window seat. (The shadows of leaves on the wall also have to
do with that translation.) My brother is heard teaching his
grandchildren a Glasgow counting-out rhyme which my
mother taught to us when we were young. The Salvation
Army band is a familiar sound to be heard from the house,
and the last post is from an Armistice Day (my birthday)
parade (the building of the war memorial being something
that was seen from the window of an earlier house, in early
childhood – the exciting thing on the Kirk Green then being to
me the big crane lifting the stones, so that I understood 'war
memorial' as referring to it). The carrying out of furniture is
made to seem rather sad by the accompaniment of a
lugubrious pop song. And the 'bones' of the house are revealed
as it empties. I mean these things to give a sort of texture,
without necessarily knowing what it all comes out of.
(Margaret Tait — Imagined Interview)

Stills, *Place of Work* and *Tailpiece*

Aspects of Kirkwall

Kirkwall is my home town, and I hadn't realised how
'photogenic' it is until I saw some local newsreel material
which Douglas Shearer used to shoot and then show in The
Phoenix, in Kirkwall. That was many years ago, and it gave
me the idea I'd like to try and describe the town on film. Now
I have made five films which I group together as *Aspects of
Kirkwall*; but I've missed out a lot of things, and I don't feel I
have really described the town yet. But they are films. They
are pictures, with townscape as their starting-off point, and
'description' is really no longer what they are, at all. The last
two: *The Look of the Place* and *Some Changes* ... spanned a
number of years in what you see. Some editing ideas took
time to develop. So although in *The Look of the Place* there
are some scenes shot in 1969, and the latest scene to be
filmed for it was 1976 ... it wasn't actually dubbed and
printed until 1981. So that even while I was still working on
it, in the end I was looking back, to how some things in the
town had looked, but no longer looked. This, I suppose, is
what led me to call the next one *Some Changes*. I was picking
up things which either had changed or suggested change to
come, or which gave a sort of 'changed days' atmosphere. Of
course there are echoes of *On the Mountain* in all this. (to TK)

On 'stalking the image'

I found this expression about 'stalking the image'. That's
Lorca in a tercentenary lecture about Don Luis de Gongora.
And he also says "for Gongora, an apple is no less intense
than the sea, a bee no less astonishing than a forest." "He
takes all materials in the same scale", and "the Poet must
know this," Lorca says. The kind of cinema that I care about
is on that level, of poetry, and I might say in a way that my
life's work has consisted of making film poems. Of course,
when I started doing medicine, I thought that medicine would
be my life's work, but at a certain – I think I gradually came
over to feeling that it was necessary to do something more
than just simply bringing people back to bodily health, and
got into this other realm. (to TK)

Stills, *Aspects of Kirkwall* (from left to right) *The Look of the Place, Shape of the Town, Some Changes, The Ba', Occasions*

On recording

You asked me, the other day, about making records of things.
I'm not really interested in 'recording for posterity'. That's an
incidental, or accidental, value that my films might have, not
what I'm making them for. I make my films for audiences who
are there at the time – for a response, at the time. I would
hope, anyway, that there's more to it than just: 'Oh look!
That's such-and-such a place' or 'Here, isn't that Mr. So-and-
So in that shot', even though I do like bringing those things
in. In my use of the language of film, I do show things like
that – sometimes – and if I am using them I like to have them
accurate; but more for the sake of reverberation than for
the sake of record.

Some film makers have a sort of diary approach. But that
is not what I am intending, even if it seems like that because
of my daily excursions to collect material, over a period of
time. When I've got the material I'm looking for, I stop. It's
not random, really; it's not just anything that happens, 'that's
what happened to me today'. No.

The photographs, then – all 24 of them in every second –
and the recorded sounds – are the equivalent of notes, or
works (or letters might be nearer it) or blobs of paint, and it's
a matter of composing them so that the effect is in a sense
musical – or poetic, if that's a better word for it.

It's mysterious, isn't it? That photographs joined together and passing in front of you in the order that they do – at the same time as a track of sounds is heard – can produce this effect. Because you can readily create the illusion of movement – the phenomenon that all cinema is based on, after all – there's no end to how you can use that phenomenon to create a piece of work.

Sure, there's a sort of historical interest in seeing film which has survived from a former time, showing how things used to be, as there is an exotic interest in seeing things on film from some other part of the world. But that in itself isn't very much. Recording for its own sake is an educative, or journalistic, use of film, (worthy enough in its way) that has the same relation to the kind of filmmaking that I care about as textbooks or newspapers have to literature. (to TK)

An art of the country

And this is something too about working in Scotland ... I
maybe started making films in another country – in Italy –
but the sort of film that arises out of your own country ...
reverberates back to the people in it, who belong to that place
too. Then this comes back into the film again. This was
something that was happening in Italy in the early fifties.
They suddenly found that they were making films which sort
of surged up out of the place, out of themselves and how they
felt about things ... I mean a true art of the country, now this
does seem to be kind of lacking in Scotland. (to JW)

On the avant-garde

I was asked to exhibit at Film London [the 1979 Festival of
Avant-Garde Film] but I never describe my work as avant-
garde. I don't see that it's a term one can use of oneself
anyway. How can anyone say such a thing of themself?
Besides that, there's something too limiting about the idea
of avant-garde – as if at all costs you must be making
innovations. Cinema itself is an innovation of this century,
and within the mainstream of it, the most astonishing
things have been achieved. It bowls me over. It really does.

**But do you mind your films being called avant-
garde – by others? ...**

Oh, well, no! How could I mind that? It's not the only thing
they've been called, though. (to TK)

On seeing

I peer at things, I really peer at things through my camera
viewfinder … I do sometimes actually use it to help me see
the thing, you know. I frame it for myself through the
viewfinder and see it differently. It's not just the framing. It's
something else you see [that comes] of looking through a lens.
You peer at it more closely I think; follow it. And this is partly
why I have developed a habit of using the camera hand held,
because earlier on I wouldn't have dreamt of taking it off the
tripod, you know. I wasn't exactly taught to do that, but you
sort of take it in that the camera should be firmly on the
tripod. But, there's a shot in *Orquil Burn* which led me to
this. It was just a particular little bit of following the water
running along and at a certain moment some little beetle or
something gets on maybe just a leaf, gets caught in the
current and goes whipping up into some pods that are at the
side of the burn, and I was able to follow it, you see, and it
just made all the difference to that thing. In fact somehow or
other it forms the whole film, that particular shot, so I felt the
more I could get of this the better.

And using a handheld camera obviously you can
sometimes just get round the corner, so to speak. (to JW)

The camera

Just what are the limitations you have to work with?
Well, they are of two kinds really. One is from working alone
in a sense. I mean not just having a group of people around to
do the different things such as sort of trying to pick up
everything at once. The other is just the actual camera I use
is a lightweight clockwork Bolex, so that the end, of course,
only runs a certain length, and the [film] roll is only of a
certain length, but I have a hundred feet to work with before
I have to change the film, and about eighteen feet or
something like that in one wind. So that – yes – it does
eventually influence the way that I compose the films, even
on paper before I start. The fact that I know that I have to
work in short takes. And I know that I'm going to have to
work in short takes before I ever start.

**And how do you deal with the people who appear
in the film?**
I think I've always felt that I'd like to introduce the
atmosphere of somebody being there behind the camera, as
well as there being people in front of the camera. And maybe
you always feel this in a film anyway; maybe it's a bit naïve
to think that you have to deliberately bring it in … But I'm
sometimes physically in the film myself … you'll see my
shadow appears holding the camera. (to JW)

On sound recording / mixing

The Big Sheep, for instance, is joined entirely end to end with
the sound lab simply adjusting the balance between different
bits, not having to mix the sound together ... I liked the idea
of natural sound; whatever else was mixed in with them, so
that since I acquired a tape recorder of my own less than four
years ago [1974], I've been able to work out the sounds at an
earlier stage. I mean practically work them out, rather than
just theoretically. My picture-sync has just one magnetic
track. So I have to lay each track separately. You can see on
the cue-sheet where you are obviously, but I can't play [the
different tracks] together, not here I mean. I could go
somewhere else and play them before I finally got it mixed. I
should do that I suppose, but sometimes I quite like relying
on – I mean you have to exercise your imagination a bit more
strongly when you're doing the separate tracks. You have to
be absolutely sure of each thing, and not trust to just a
general mush to carry it over. (to JW)

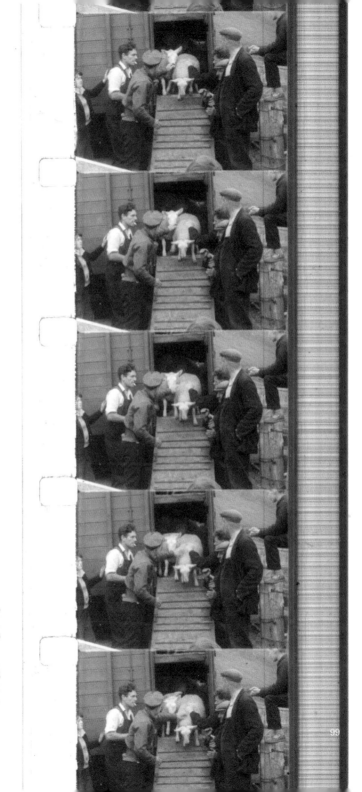

Filmstrip, *The Big Sheep*

Still, *Tailpiece*

Preserving the Margaret
Tait Film Collection

Some months after the death of Margaret Tait in 1999, the
Scottish Screen Archive was approached by her husband, Alex
Pirie, with a proposal for deposit of all the film material that
had been amassed in Orquil Studio, a converted kirk
purchased by Tait in 1984.

The collection of some 150 cans of film arrived in
consignments between October 1999 and October 2000, Alex
taking the evening ferry from Stromness across the Pentland
Firth and driving through the night to arrive at the Archive
in Glasgow just as we were opening for business at the start
of the day – emptying the boot of his small car full of rusty
cans of 16mm film.

The importance of the collection was immediate. We knew
of Margaret Tait, indeed the Archive Curator had, over
previous years, unsuccessfully approached her with regard to
preserving her collection. Alex was not surprised at this.
Margaret, he recalled, worked in the present, making films
which she regarded as artefacts belonging to the time in
which they were made. She knew the value of her works and
wanted them to be shown as widely as possible. But she

seems to have taken few steps to maintain her negatives and prints. 'Posterity' was something she gave little thought to.

We were excited by the acquisition of the collection, one of the most significant collections to be received by Scotland's national moving image archive. Although unique in many respects, Tait's collection does sit within a pattern of film-making in Scotland as reflected in the Scottish Screen Archive. Until recent times indigenous Scottish film culture has been predominantly non-fiction, a cluster of documentary, sponsored, educational, industrial and ethnographic filmmaking that reflects the influence of John Grierson. History has benefited from what are now archival collections of moving images that provide testimony and evidence of the real Scotland in the film century – in contrast to the external stereotypical fictional screen representation of Scottishness that audiences have almost come to expect. Tait sits within that culture of non-fiction with her observational films such as *Rose Street* and her chronicling over the years of the traditions of the Kirkwall Ba' game.

Margaret Tait was an independent in the truest sense, intriguingly in common with her fellow women director / photographers in Scottish film history. Like Tait, they mostly worked alone, outwith the structures of the film industry, recording communities on the island fringes (Tait in Orkney, Jenny Gilbertson in Shetland, Margaret Fay Shaw in the Uists), visiting and recording societies often difficult to get to (Isobel Wylie Hutchinson travelling by coast guard steamer to Greenland in the 1920s, 75-year old Gilbertson filming in the Canadian Arctic), working and living within societies where women's roles were defined and constrained in traditional activities (unmarried Jenny Gilbertson scandalising local society in the 1930s by taking off on her own, with camera and tent, on filming expeditions to the remoter parts of Shetland). Equally, Margaret Tait stands out as an individual in Scottish film for her work outwith the factual. Reprising perhaps the experimental work of Norman McLaren at Glasgow School of Art in the 1930s with hand painting on to film stock and mixing live action with animation, her experimental work and highly visual film poems are far removed from the main body of production in Scotland. They have an international critical standing that few Scottish film makers in history have achieved. As such hers is a collection that at one level reinforces a Scottish tradition in film, but equally challenges and pushes out its boundaries into new forms.

Preserving the collection

The first task of the preservation was a technical examination of the contents of the cans. Reel by reel, the film conservator undertook a bench inspection of the material, noting its physical condition and the extent of the damage (for example: tears, badly made and dried out film joins, scratches, perforation damage, shrinkage, film base distortion, colour fading, fungus growth and the chemical breakdown of the film base itself). It was discovered that all of the damage already described was present throughout the collection. This was not unusual considering the number of film cans. There were, however, problems discovered that were unique to Margaret's films and never encountered before by the Archive. Most alarming was the evidence that original copies (sometimes the only existing copy of a work) had been used as projection prints, resulting in original negatives being scratched, and damaged.

The conditions of storage in the island studio had not been kind to the films – dampness was the main problem. This was compounded by the fact that the film maker had an 'individual' relationship with film laboratories. (Early in her film career a laboratory mislaid the negative of *Rose Street*. It has never been found.) She preferred that all original material and printing masters be returned to her studio instead of being placed into store in laboratory vaults, as is customary. As a result, all the elements of the film, such as camera reversals and negatives, not just the presentation copies that film makers would normally have in their possession, were affected by damp and mould.

An array of experimental and non-conventional filmmaking techniques, such as: painting and scratching on the film's surface, splicing negative and positive film stocks together within one title, and effects compounded by the ravages of time and the environment, made preserving the Margaret Tait collection one of the most challenging projects faced by the Scottish Screen Archive. Ethical considerations have been endlessly discussed in the planning of how to undertake the duplication work. It has not always been clear what the film maker intended – what might seem to a laboratory grader today to be a technical fault to be remedied in the duplication process, might in fact have been an intentional effect that the film maker wanted to create.

During the restoration of the Tait collection frequent problems arose regarding image and sound quality. Existing projection copies (prints) can be used as a guide to help the conservator achieve a new print from an original negative that replicates the look of the prints previously presented by the film maker. Grading information i.e. how light or dark each scene was printed, and how the film was edited, can be found on the existing prints in a collection. When a film is printed for the first time (answer print) it may be accepted by the film maker, or he or she may ask for alterations to be made. The film maker may want to change the colour of a scene, make a scene darker or lighter or adjust the sound levels, etc. The lab will then reprint the film using the film maker's instructions to produce a print that is acceptable to them.

Tait's work did cause unconventional problems, however, because existing prints from one title all looked different. These differences could be subtle and difficult to spot. For instance, with *The Big Sheep* there were two 16mm prints. On one a whole scene had been physically removed, and the presence of splices told that the other had had two scenes shortened. Neither print was the same length as the negative from which it was made. Was that particular scene removed from one print copy because Tait had changed her mind and re-edited the film, or was the sequence removed at a later date as a running repair to a damaged copy? At the end of

Aerial is a sunset, shot in black and white. On one print Tait had coloured it in using paints applied direct on to the 16mm stock. A third print would appear to be a duplicate made from that painted copy, the colours subtly different to the original.

We talked to lab staff who had worked on Tait's films with her. Martin Sawyer has vivid recollections of a film maker who was very particular about how her film looked and had very firm ideas of what she was creating as a visual expression. He can remember how she would become frustrated when told that the duplicating processes could not readily deliver the effects that she visualised and that printing equipment could not always cope with the physical methods she used in making her films. The labs wanted to help and would try coming up with ways around the problem. Initially unhappy about the extra cost this incurred she would usually be happy with the results. Unintentional errors could become effects – an out of focus scene, which was difficult to print up, was then left in as an effect, which she found she quite liked. On one version of

Painted Eightsome is written across the frames 'NO NO NO'. Is this a reproduction result she was unhappy with, or an effect?

This knowledge of her relationship with the laboratories and reference to the surviving prints in the collection helps determine the accuracy of the films' restoration. As there were some titles with several prints each contained slight differences, we decided to recreate the last version, which the laboratory printed and was accepted by Tait, where we could determine what that was. The subtle visual differences between various prints are all recorded by the Archive, so that the alternative versions can be restored if required.

Early on in the technical inspection we were alerted by the labelling on several cans to the fact that they contained examples of original hand painted material. Closer examination confirmed this. 35mm clear stock with paints painstakingly applied by brush, frame by frame, directly on to the celluloid. An unusual problem was therefore posed – how best to preserve and duplicate these extraordinary pieces of work?

Paint on Film: restoring Calypso

Calypso is customarily dated 1955, although evidence would suggest that this, Tait's first experiment with painting on to film stock, was first created in Italy three years earlier. Peter Hollander, her fellow student at the Centro Sperimentale di Cinematografia, recalled that Margaret was given a surplus piece of 35mm soundtrack with calypso music on it by a technical officer at the office of the British Information Service in Rome. A nitrate test reel, in a can labelled 'hand painted in Rome', was discovered by Alex Pirie in Margaret's studio in October 2002.

Calypso is a painted film on clear 35mm film stock with optical sound track. Each frame / image was painted on to the film by hand using a brush and colour dyes. Margaret had used dyes which are water soluble. This presented a major problem, in that most preservation and restoration techniques use a wet process such as cleaning, re-washing or wet gate printing. As the dyes on *Calypso* will dissolve in water these techniques could not be applied.

It is important that a film restoration tries to duplicate an original as accurately as possible. Recreating today the colours of the original painted film would be very difficult to achieve. The aniline dyes used in *Calypso* and the photographic dyes used today to create the colour image on colour film stock are different. So how do we copy and match the colours accurately? First, to prevent damage to the original we decided to create a test roll. By happy coincidence the film conservator who was working on the collection with us at the time was an experienced art restorer. Using her knowledge of paints and dyes, and with research into Margaret's writings, she was able to establish what kind of dyes had been used. The type of medical aniline dyes used in the original in the 1950s were very difficult to obtain today, therefore, we experimented with similar dyes that were readily available. Although they were not an exact match they would be adequate to enable the creation of a short test roll. The test roll consisted of 57 frames painted using similar

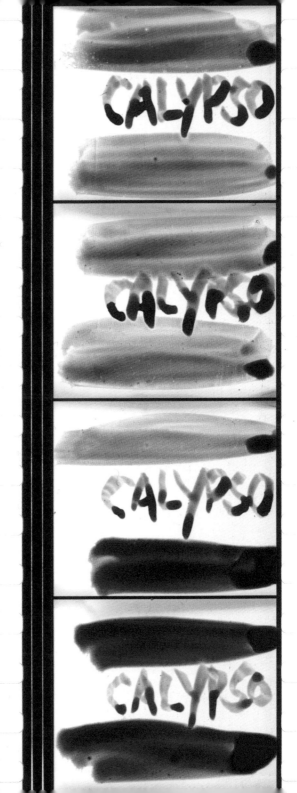

Filmstrip, *Calypso*

motifs and colours which appeared on the original. This test roll was then sent to the film laboratory and a new internegative and print were made. The results, although promising, did not really match the colours painted on the original. We therefore concluded that the true reproduction of the colours in *Calypso* would be difficult using this method of duplication.

We approached the bfi National Film and Television Archive with a proposal for a collaborative restoration. The NFTVA's then Conservation Officer, Joao Socrates De Oliveira, had had previous experience of preserving painted celluloid, having restored Len Lye's *Colour Box* (1935). He became an enthusiastic partner in our project. It was decided to try three different preservation paths on *Calypso* and after comparing the results of each we could then decide on the best method to use for preserving the other hand-painted titles in the collection.

The three methods selected were:

1. Scanning the original images and utilising computer software to digitally restore the image and remove image scratches and blemishes and then re-record back on to 35mm film.

2. Making a new colour internegative and print with colour correction.

3. Making black and white positives from the original film using red, green and blue filters and then using these black and white separations, combined with the RGB filters, to make a new colour print. (This method is the preferred path for colour preservation but is the most expensive.)

As testing is still in progress (June 2004) the results obtained so far are as expected – no one single path can match the original colours exactly. The colour internegative produces the closest match to the colours in the original. The digital path has produced the cleanest image, as the scratches have been reduced greatly with digital restoration, but the colour is not as close. At the time of writing we still await the outcome of the black and white separation test, but the prediction is that this path will also produce slightly different colour from the colours found on the original.

A record is kept by the Archive of all duplication work, to compare the physical quality of the new copies with the original. Nothing that has been done is irreversible. The original film is preserved in its original state. At the time of writing the restoration of the complete set of six hand-painted films has only just begun.

$\sim\!/\backslash\!\!\!\!\!\!\!\!\!\!\!\!\!\sim$

Calypso, digitally restored, was premiered at Edinburgh International Film Festival in August 2004.

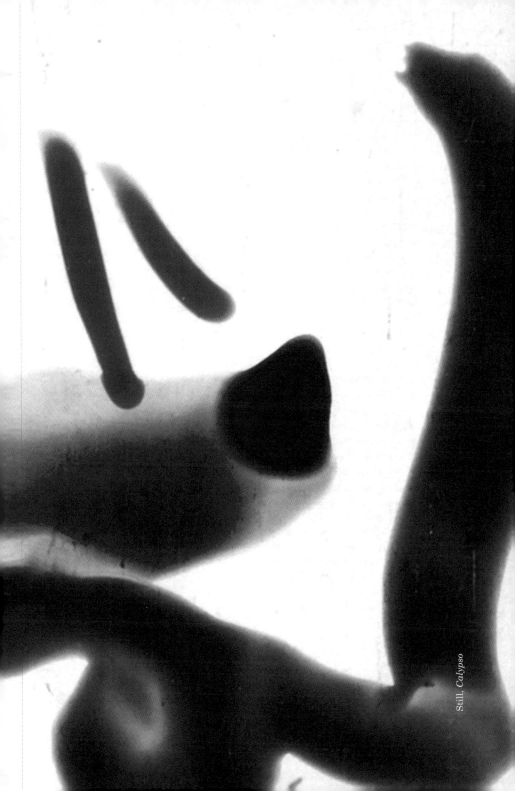

Still, *Calypso*

Still, *Calypso*

Still, *Painted Eightsome*

Poems, stories, texts

Poems, stories, texts

As well as making films, Margaret Tait wrote two books of short stories, *Lane Furniture* (1959) and *The Grassy Stories* (1959), and three books of poetry: *Origins and Elements* (1959), *Subjects and Sequences* (1960) and *The Hen and the Bees* (1960).

This section reproduces a small selection of poems, a short story and other selected writings and artworks. Also included is a letter concerning the sound mix for *On the Mountain*, which gives an insight into her process as a film maker working at a physical distance from film labs or sound studios.

from Origins and Elements

To Anybody at All

I didn't want you cosy and neat and limited.
I didn't want you to be understandable,
Understood.
I wanted you to stay mad and limitless,
Neither bound to me nor bound to anyone else's or
    your own preconceived idea of yourself.

Elasticity

Think of the word, elastic.
The real elastic quality is the being able to spring back
    to the original shape,
Not the being able to be stretched.
So, metal is described as elastic
And steel is the most elastic of all metals.
It is specially manufactured to have the elastic quality
    of retaining its own shape.
Steel is so elastic you can't budge it.

Now

I used to lie in wait to see the clover open
Or close,
But never saw it.
I was too impatient,
Or the movement is too subtle,
Imperceptible
And more than momentary.
My five-year-old self would tire of waiting
And when I looked again
– All closed for the night!
I missed it
Once more.

Cinematographically
I have registered the opening of escholtzia
On an early summer morning.
It gave me a sharp awareness of time passing,
Of exact qualities and values in the light,
But I didn't see the movement
As movement.
I didn't with my own direct perception see the petals
    moving.
Later, on the film, they seemed to open swiftly,
But, at the time,
Although I stared
And felt time not so much moving as being moved in
And felt
A unity of time and place with other times and places
Yet
I didn't see the petals moving.
I didn't see them opening.
They were closed,
And later they were open,
And in between I noted many phases,
But I didn't see them moving open.
My timing and my rhythm could not observe the
    rhythm of their opening.

The thing about poetry is you have to keep doing it.
People have to keep making it.
The old stuff is no use
Once it's old.
It comes out of the instant
And lasts for an instant.
            Take it now
            Quickly
            Without water.

There!

    Tomorrow there'll be something else.

The atoms are exploding throughout our atmosphere.
A bombardment
Of rays reaches our innards,
But we don't know it.
Like crazy delinquents
Whose moment is worth so little
That they use it to destroy the next one
We set off a crackling and a popping of all we are
    made of,
Liberating the final rays that held us together
But which,
Liberated and lost,
Can only split us
And disintegrate our several cells and entire selves.

No one should ever get to think of themselves as
    infallible
Or of anyone else as infallible.
We are all capable of folly.

So let me even praise unwisdom a little,
For we are never so wise
As to be all-wise;
And in discarding all wisdom and prudence
Now and again,
– Rarely, say, but still sometimes –
We can reach,
We can see,
We can feel, touch, sense in some indefinable way
A deeper knowledge than wisdom,
    Bone-knowledge
      Blood-knowledge
        Felt or known by our deepest sensibilities
For which as yet we have no words.

from The Hen and the Bees

Light
Did you say it's made of waves?
Yes, that's it.
I wonder what the waves are made of.
Oh, waves are made of waves.
Waves are what they are,
Shimmeringness,
Oscillation,
Rhythmical movement which is the inherent essence
    of all things.
Ultimately, there's only movement,
Nothing else.
The movement that light is
Comes out of the sun
And it's so gorgeous a thing
That nothing else is ever anything unless lit by it.

Trust
I like you to extend out in all your endless
    possibilities.
I like you to inhabit the multitudes you contain.
I like to know that a lot of your being is away beyond
    me
As a lot of me is beyond you.
The trust relates to that part,
To the unknown.
I trust you to know or feel what to do with your own
    unknown,
And I trust you to trust me to be in the me unknown
    to you honest and not in the end forgetful of you.

Loki Beside the Standing Stone

One of the gods, called Loki,
Not very popular with the others,
Sat against a stone, and pondered.
The stone was one of a circle
Raised
By men in honour of something they didn't understand.
Loki neither
Understood,
But he liked the feeling of the great stone behind him,
Rough with jagged crumbly lichen
And warm, in a way, from the sun,
Yet inwardly cold, cold as a stone keeps inwardly cold
    in the north;
And as he sat there, pressing his back against the flat
    stone,
Some comfort came from it
And he felt less hopeless
About his own tiresome tendency
To play pranks which somehow always ended in
    disaster.
He realised
That if that was really his inherent character
He had to keep on like that
And never mind if nobody liked him.

For Using

Material things are only tools
Or they're nothing.
Food is a sort of tool,
Fire a warming tool,
And paint-brushes, pencils, cameras, books
All tools of a kind
For making a life
Or lives.
But too much food is poison,
Comfort a permanent anaesthetic,
And too many paint-brushes, cameras, books
Waste away as toys.
A tool has the feel of the user's hand on it
If it's a real tool.
A tool that is fully used
Gets a bloom on it
From its own essential-ness.
All other bits and things are clutter.

from Subjects and Sequences

Bushels
Women under bushels,
Extinguished lights,
Women poets
–Poetesses–
You never had a chance, had you?

They either dressed you in blue stockings
Or put you in the kitchen.
You could be gracious
    or gossipy
    or good cooks,
"Motherly,"
Or, if not that, then "manly," they insisted,
Never strong, feminine, yourselves,
Not that, never that,
Never women, poetesses,
Beings and doers in your own right.

Miss Bayne
"There's been
a terrible lot of accidents this year,"
said Miss Bayne of Dunblane.
"Heavens! A Blind Woman
Run Over By A Train,"
exclaims my mother.
I like this spontaneous concern
for anonymous unfortunates,
and I would like to think that when I do expire
some unknown stranger for me might spare a sigh.

Mary, Queen of Scots

Mary came dancing.
Oh, what a crime!
Mary was entrancing, –
A sin in the eyes of the Lord.
The black-coated gentlemen
Knew fine the Lord's wishes in the matter.
Well they knew
That ladies are not for decoration nor for pleasure
And certainly not for any activity of the mind
Other than serving
Their lords and masters,
Men
Made in the image of God.

Women were not made in the image of anything,
Because of course there is no Goddess for them to be made in
    the image of,
Only a God
With a voice like thunder
  – Or soft spoken when he appears on earth in the form of
    his own Son –
And a long white beard
Or a wispy black one, according to which is more suitable in
    the circumstances.

So Mary was supposed to squash herself
Into the man-made corsets
Of staid deportment,
Seemly deference to her statesmen
And ear-drum-shattering demands that she change her church
    IMMEDIATELY

Mary was young.
She imagined life was for enjoying.
She imagined that sensible people would listen to her.
But she was wrong.

I wonder what she did to pass the time, all those years in
  prison.
She must have been relieved, in the end, to get her head
  cut off.

from Lane Furniture

Sixteen Frames Per Second

The little boy stared and stared at the immense silent hooves on the screen above him, and although he was about dropping with sleep he couldn't take his eyes off them. Beside him, his mother played away resoundingly on the upright piano. He knew the music she was playing as intimately as he knew his mother's own moods and could almost tell by the way she played just what story he would have at bed-time and certainly whether she would be loving and dilatory or brisk and rather distant as she sometimes was.

The mother was entirely taken up in her adult and exacting occupation, and so the little boy was quite alone, related neither to the immense spectres on the screen nor to the jolly crowd out there, all facing the screen and laughing up at it as they followed the pranks of images they knew. He was in between, and could watch either as he chose. Usually he chose to watch the grey abstractions rather than the smelly, laughing, coughing humans in rows beyond the balustrade and the pot plants.

One night, though, he had watched a little boy rather younger than himself who sat in the very front row between his handsome young parents. The boy was young to be out for an evening's entertainment, and really it appeared as if he might have been taken along only because the parents wanted to be there and could not leave him at home alone. At first he sat in his own seat, frowning a little at the incomprehensible figures on the screen, and playing at tipping his seat up by changing his posture. This was found very irritating by the lady behind him, who, after a time, put a stop to it, and then the child slumped lower and lower until his father took him on his knee, and there he fell soundly asleep.

The little boy beside the piano watched the other child, who slept on his father's knee unaware of the two conflicting realities present in the theatre, much as he himself felt outside them. All through the picture he looked and looked at the boy comfortably asleep in his father's arms, supported rather as he was supported by his mother's nearness and by the steady beat of the music which she performed so sturdily.

The memory of the sleeping child among the audience did give the little boy beside the piano a dim sort of realisation that out there in that crowd which he heard and smelt but only dimly saw there must be others like himself. But being himself isolated where he was it did not occur to him that he might meet and know those others.

The wild white horse on the screen had broken out of the stockade once again, and went galloping away over the hills quite out of reach of its pursuers. The little boy then watched the giant grey figures of cowboys discussing what they would do next, and their words too appeared in gigantic letters rather too much at a slant from where he sat for him to be able to read them. The cowboys' horses were very beautiful too, but they had just been saddled and were setting out into the hills when a strange flickering took place, and blurred figures rushed vertically up the screen and into nothing. Then they stopped, and there was darkness.

For a moment his mother hesitated, then she went on playing jog-trot music for about half a minute until the lights went up.

It was like lighting a match in a cave and finding it full of people. They stretched, and moved in their seats, and many of them laughed at the physical surprise of the breakdown and then the lights. They mostly kept staring fixedly towards the screen for a few moments, but presently a general chattering began and got louder and louder. The girls selling popcorn came down the aisles and there was even a sort of joviality about the interruption.

The little boy's mother had stopped playing when the lights went on, but the manager came from a private door down near the screen and told her to play something as it would take a few minutes to put things right in the projection room. She started on some popular songs of that time, and although at first the music could hardly be heard above the hubbub of talk there were a few in the crowd who listened and even joined in with their voices. She played a hit song, and very soon the packed auditorium was filled with the not entirely tuneful singing of all those people.

The little boy, who had been examining the blankness of the screen with a certain sort of interest, turned then to watch the other spectacle, of the audience. His mother played away vivaciously, for it was stimulating for her to find the audience actually paying attention to her music. During the films she sometimes wondered if they noticed her playing at all, although of course they would notice if she stopped. So now she played the popular songs extraordinarily well, reacting to the enthusiasm of the listeners and the singers. The little boy watched the people singing, rows and rows of wide open mouths and swaying shoulders. One joker even got into the aisle and "conducted" them with flourishes of his arms.

At the end of the song there was tremendous applause. The manager reappeared.

"Something quieter," he said. "Play something quieter."

So the little boy's mother played a simple, rather sentimental tune, but one that the audience could hardly be expected to know the words of. Some stalwarts tried to sing it all the same, but the glorious unison of the popular song was gone for ever and a certain restlessness made itself felt among the crowd. There was a shuffling of feet and an occasional cry of "Hurry up, there," and "What are we waiting for?"

One little family was so grateful for the joyous song in which all the house had taken part that they came down the aisle and leaned across the balustrade to thank the pianist. She was quite touched and just continued playing rather softly and absentmindedly while she talked to them. The little boy tried to keep behind the piano and not be seen by the well-dressed lady and gentleman and by the almost grown-up boy and girl.

"You haven't got your little boy with you to-night," said the lady. "You know, we often see you together, outside, and the children say, 'There goes the wee boy from the picture-house, with his mother.' But I suppose he's home in his bed now."

"No, he's here," said the mother. "Where are you?" So the little boy had to come out and be seen.

"I do believe you were hiding," said the lady, laughing roguishly. "But I have something here for little boys who *aren't* hiding." And from her ample handbag she produced a box of sweets.

"Oh mother!" said the girl.

"Be quiet," said the lady. "We'll get more." And she handed the box to the little boy, who just gazed at it in dismay.

"Take it," said the gentleman. "They're sweets. Perhaps you don't like sweeties, eh? Ha ha ha."

"You take them for him, then," the lady said to the little boy's mother. "He's shy."

"He's sleepy," said his mother. "Thank you very much, but you shouldn't do this."

"We really appreciate your playing," said the lady's husband.

"Say thank you," the little boy's mother said to him.

"Thank you," said the little boy.

"There now, that's a good little boy," said the lady.

The lights gave a warning flicker.

"We'd better get back to our seats," said the big boy.

"Yes, hurry," said the girl.

"We'll see you again, sonny," said the lady, as they all went away. The man turned and waved to him, and he waved back, but he felt his security jangled and he hoped that his own secret situation by the piano would never again be invaded by people from the audience. It was as unfitting for that to have happened as it would have been for the black and grey figures from the screen to jump down beside him.

Then the picture started again, and his mother played trotting music as the cowboys rode over the hill, and now and again when the little boy glanced nervously towards the audience he was relieved to see that all the people were safely hidden in darkness.

Film-poem or poem-film: A Few Notes about Film and Poetry

In my 'self-made films' (what Peter Todd calls no-budget films) I'm always looking at where I am at the time, considering at length my immediate surroundings and 'making use of available actuality' as I used to say. But in the feature scripts, which are fictional, imaginary situations are what I use. (Only one of those screenplays, *Blue Black Permanent*, has so far been realised on film.) Surroundings, for fiction film, whether all sets built specifically for the film or partly 'real' – real places standing in for imaginary, places – and props made for the part or at least sought out, chosen and placed, or maybe just 'found' already there, can end up being used in much the same way; – I mean, stared at, brought into the imaginary whole along with their own actuality.

The contradictory or paradoxical thing is that in a documentary the real things depicted are liable to lose their reality by being photographed and presented in that 'documentary' way, and there's no poetry in that. In poetry, something else happens. Hard to say what it is. Presence, let's say, soul or spirit, an empathy with whatever it is that's dwelt upon, feeling for it – to the point of identification.

On the other hand, I have at times been imbued with the idea of making a film to illustrate, or to set (in the sense of setting a poem to music) an existing poem, a known poem, and an early effort of mine was to set to pictures Hopkins' "The Leaden Echo and the Golden Echo". In *Hugh MacDiarmid, A Portrait* I tried similar, by setting picture to "Somersault" and "Krang" as spoken by MacDiarmid. Different from *The Eemis Stane,* which is in the film with its musical setting, as a totality, and the picture during that is 'incidental'. Then again, when MacDiarmid reads "You Know

Not Who I Am", which opens the film and closes it, that comes as a comment on the film and what it's about and on the partiality fully to be expected of a portrait.

I think that film is essentially a poetic medium, and although it can be put to all sorts of other – creditable and discreditable – uses, these are secondary.

The great joy of directing *Blue Black Permanent* was in working with the cast and crew, each bringing their own qualities into the feeling of the whole thing. It's mainly the actors and actresses who give so much greater scope in a feature compared with a short. They and the characters they create bring it into quite a different dimension from what one can do working away by oneself with a camera and an editing bench. Even all the organisation associated with having performers affects the dimension; and one of the miracles about film is that that, and all the complications of production on a wider scale, don't have to quell the poetry that's inherent in what's being made, so long as its there in the first place.

— Margaret Tait, *Poem Film Film Poem*, No. 2, 1997

On Video Poems for the 90s

It was in the summer of 1995 when I went North to visit
Margaret Tait in the windy Orkney Islands. Two years earlier
a friend mentioned her as a personal poetic film maker who
would interest me, so when I came to London I watched all
the prints the Co-op had and was so excited about them that
we brought copies to Berlin to distribute and screen, and later
to many other places in Germany and Switzerland.

So there I was in Margaret's kirk, her studio, in an old
Orcadian church. But the most beautiful hours we shared
together were watching all the films I hadn't seen – in her
dark-green painted small living room with a golden framed
screen, the size of a painting ... the most beautiful cinema!
A moving painting!

Some days later Margaret showed me her 'script' *Video
Poems for the 90s* which she wrote after Scottish
television had asked her for a 12-minute script, but they
didn't want to realise it. Margaret thought of it as a kind of
model, which others can also use to make a film from.

She asked me if we wanted to film two *Poems for the
90s* – so we took our Bolexes, and went to the edge of the sea,
looked for rust and birds and filmed 'turning a page' ...

It was very nice working together out there in the
Orcadian countryside with Margaret Tait filming with her
Bolex, which she hadn't used for a long time, because she was
so much involved in her 35mm film *Blue Black Permanent*
and now she was working on a new script, also for a 35mm
feature long film ...

We didn't finish the film poems, but it was an
unforgettable beginning ... with no end.

— Ute Aurand

Video Poems for the 90s (working title)

With Celtic art – Celtic culture very much in mind. i.e. (inc.) the end in the beginning, the beginning in the end (e.g. intertwined serpents with the head swallowing the tail) in so much of Celtic design – jewellery, book illumination, crosses, stonework ...

Animated title using this design idea – then nine themes, interlocking:

1. A child reading – a 'simple' image, contemplating the intent way in which a young child reads, or looks at a book, meeting the world of storybook or picture book. Hold it – Hold it simple – Hold it direct.

2. The edge of the sea. Literally the very edge where shore meets water – life on both sides. [Here Margaret Tait has a little drawing of edge of the sea, a symbol, but also a reality.]

3. Birds in wilderness – ("Here we sit like birds in the wilderness") Real birds – Real wilderness. ("In and out the dusty bluebells") (Melancholic bird calls) (Bees)

4. Stock on the Road. Touch of incongruity, touch of "what are they doing there?" whiff of ineffable sadness (if not tragedy) in the fate of all creatures – Insistence through several instances of stock-moving, stock straying or finding its way out – or being driven along willy-nilly –

5. Rust everywhere. Plenty of instances of this. Rather inanimate, rather static, but, nevertheless, implied in the crumbling machinery the dwindled fencing and gateposts is that nothing stays the same.

6. Heavy Traffic – Oh, yes! Far from rusted yet. The maintained, the oiled, the useful, the busy.

7. Flight to and from – comes out of six – articulated lorries entering the ferry, heavy car doors, the leaving and the arriving – Aircraft, different sizes, up and away, down and in – Sailboats and other boats – A busy scene – Where do they all come from? Where are they all going? The birds too, they flock and wheel and prepare to leave. Flight of individual birds.

8. Crash of a wave – a direct statement – An irrefutable image –

9. Turning a page. The quiet page turning by the grown person – (with echoes perhaps of a device in many film titles).

Then animated decoration again in the end titles.

— Margaret Tait

ANCO

FILMS

ANCONA FILMS

BUTTQUOY HOUSE
KIRKWALL
ORKNEY
KW15 1JJ   Tel: KIRKWALL 3163
(STD 0856)

~~also at~~
~~SLOW BEND~~ ~~HELMSDALE~~ ~~SUTHERLAND~~

10⁰

31 May 1974

for the attention of John Maxwell,

United Motion Pictures (London) Limited,
36/38 Fitzroy Square,
London, W1P 5LL

Dear Mr. Maxwell,

ON THE MOUNTAIN

I got the edge-track striped print on Tuesday of last week . Unfortunately, I was
unable to play it for a day or two because of trouble with the Magnetic Play on my
projector. However, I have now listened to it several times. There are four points,
or perhaps five.

   1.) An extraneous noise in the first fanfare, at 10 feet : it's probable that
I accidentally caused this in the print by trying to get the Mag. Play to function.
But if it is in the original track, and the master, well, it would need to be taken
afresh from the disc, which is Boosey and Hawkes § 0.2263 ("Five Short Fanfares
for Newsreels). I can send you the disc, if you haven't got it.

okay

250 ✳
264.
construction

   2.) The whistling which you added because my track ran out: I had laid the
two sections of whistling very carefully opposite a) the gap in the harmonica
playing and b) the end of the harmonica, and it only occurs to me now that in
reducing the length of some music earlier in the track I must have forgotten to go
back and check the placing of the whistling. What you have added works all right
for the first bit, repeating what the harmonica was playing, i.e. "That's my weakness
now"; but, the second time, I don't like it at all that the whistler repeats what
was being played. (The little section I put in was "Why tell them all the old things?"
from "Whispering Grass".) Since there is plenty on the track there, without the
whistling, it would be better left out. Can the section 250 to 264 feet be done
again, and inserted, i.e. a section of construction noises only, without the
whistling, after the harmonica stops ?

NO

   3.) At the start of Part II, at 333½ feet in the whole print, the first three
[19 feet in Part II]
words of the child's song are lost. It would be better to bring it right in, without
a fade, so as not to lose the words "on the mountain".

   4.) The bit from 1062 to 1082½ in the whole print (214 -236 of Part III)
doesn't work very well. I'd rather,now, leave out track 2 altogether there and mix
tracks 1 and 3 only, that would be from 214 to 246 of Part III   , street noises on
track 1 and the child singing on track 3 and miss out the adult humming and singing
on track 2 altogether.

   5.) I'm not very happy about my use of the accordeon in Part III at 45½ to 72
feet. - or at least 46 to 70 - and I think it would be better to have 24 feet
of not too noisy street sounds in there.   In fact, I think I should
send you an alternative piece for that section. See over

Registered Office: ~~31 Rose Street Edinburgh EH2 3DX~~ - (Margaret Tait)

ANCONA FILMS

BUTTQUOY HOUSE
KIRKWALL
ORKNEY

Tel: KIRKWALL 3163

also at

SLOW BEND - HELMSDALE - SUTHERLAND

Could you advise me, please, whether these items would necessitate
a complete new mix or whether they could be added in.   The track is fine,
has mixed very well, apart from the particulav things I have enumerated.

In answer to your queries, the picture negatives are at Filmatic; Parts
I and III are Eastman colour neg. 7254,with some b & w neg among it, all to
be printed in colour positive.   Part II is a b & w dupe negative (duplicated
by Filmatic on a Kodak stock) and is to be printed on black and white positive.

I have been in touch with Mr. B.R. Pritchard at Filmatic about this
film, all along.
About no. 5.) overleaf, there should be a seagull heard in the flm
somewhere, because, perhaps paradoxically, that is one of the sounds of Rose
Street, (I think I have a section on tape that would be suitable, but I suppose
it could be done by adding just two or three seagull calls from disc above
light traffic sounds of the"magazine"variety.)   and that would be a good place
for it, instead of the accordeon, which really doesn't sound right there when
I hear the mixed track.

I agree with you that the track as mixed, at the end, is better than
the alternative ending in the separate tin.

Yours sincerely,

Margaret Tait

One of Tait's many detailed letters to the lab, here about the sound edit for
On the Mountain

Registered Office, 1 Melville Street, Edinburgh EH2 3TR   (Margaret Tait)

HUGH MACDIARMID : A PORTRAIT   1964

"A study of the poet, who was seventy-one at the time.
are 'You Know Not Who I Am', 'Somersault','Krang' and so
Kind of Poetry I Want'. The music is Francis George Sco
'The Eemis Stane', sung by Duncan Robertson, accompanied
Ogston." - M.T.

Hugh MacDiarmid – A Portrait, 1964, 9 mins.

"...she giv
ageing Scot
burn? It m
this poet,
poet George

Hugh Macdiarmid, A Portrait 1964

Script, camera, edited, produced, directed by Margaret Tait. Music by Francis George Scott. Singer: Duncan Robertson. Piano: Olive Ogdon. Poems by Hugh MacDiarmid spoken by C. M. Grieve. 9 mins.

The poems heard
out of 'The
ting of MacDiarmid's
piano by Olive

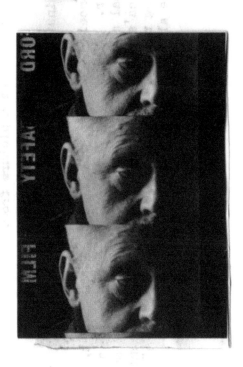

..And the bard emerges as a warm and affectionate subject, saying more and seeing more in its nine minutes than a half hour of television reportage.

Murray Grigor
Edinburgh Film Festival , 1970

subject a bold, original treatment. Why does she have the
et walk teeteringly atop a wall, and throw stones across a
o demonstrate how poised and perilous and daring is the art of
lt in homely things as well as in vast cosmic themes." - the
Brown writing in 'The Orcadian', 13 December 1979

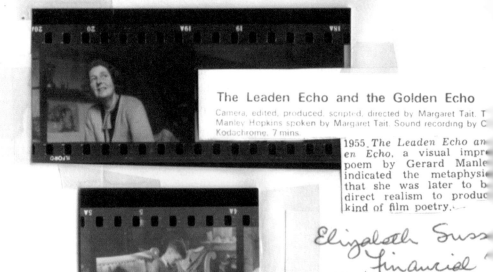

The Leaden Echo and the Golden Echo

Camera, edited, produced, scripted, directed by Margaret Tait. T
Manley Hopkins spoken by Margaret Tait. Sound recording by C
Kodachrome. 7 mins.

1955. The Leaden Echo an
en Echo, a visual impre
poem by Gerard Manle
indicated the metaphysi
that she was later to b
direct realism to produc
kind of film poetry.

Elizabeth Suss
Financial
reviewing EIFF

Glasg

FILMS AND POETRY BY MARGARET TAIT

2nd M

What the four films in this programme have in common is a us
poetry. Many of my films have no words in them at all, the
in the image, in the collocation of images and relating of t
and musical sounds. Because of this, I felt like presenting
together, along with my reading of other poetry.

THE LEADEN ECHO AND THE GOLDEN ECHO
(1955   7 minutes   colour)

A setting to images of the Hopkins poem.

This is an early film of mine - started in 1948, set aside an
and again, and completed in 1955 - in which I tried matching
the poem by Gerard Manley Hopkins. When it came to editing,
recording, first, and the picture fitted, because I had had
mind at the time of shooting; and I think I had to insert onl
pre-recorded track.

955
erard
Ltd.

the

(1970)

Theatre

9

oken words of
being entirely
natural sounds
four films

lasgow,
ALONG WITH
IECE
POEMS '74
MACDIARMID
PORTRAIT

rned to now
of my own to
the poem, for
evant lines in
pause in the

ANCONA FILM

MARGARET TAIT

WHERE I AM IS HERE 1963-4

"Starting with a six-line script which just noted down a __kind__ ef
and recur, my aim was to construct a film with its own logic, it
ences within itself, its own echoes and rhymes and comparisons,
exploration of the everyday, the commonplace, in the city, Edinb
stayed at the time.

The music, '__Hilltop pibroch__' by Hector MacAndrew, is a setting o
that name, and it is played on the fiddle by Hector himself, and
music-hall artiste, Lilane (Lilian Gunn), who accompanies hersel
accordion." -- M.T.

The seven titles within the film are:

COMPLEX

HERE AND NOW

INTERLUDE

CROCODILE

COME AND SEE THIS

OUT OF THIS WORLD

THE F

Where I Am is Here uses methods of poetry and painting to
tell the stoniness and beauty of a city. The city is Edinburgh and the
poet is Margaret Tait. She evokes, from the interaction of seeming
prosaic images of the present and a haunting soundtrack, precisely
those elements of dream, mystery, foreboding and wonder that enable
her to understand its meaning for her.

Murray Grigor
Edinburgh Film Festival 1970

The crit
framing
quiet an

occur,
respond-
gh close
re I

of
the
piano

OAT

Where I Am is Here has none of the obvious shots of Edinburgh, and a cold, sad, essentially Scottish strangeness; the dream of a city as it flows in the blood-stream of the people who live in it. Scripted, photographed and edited by Margaret Tait, its superb and intricate construction demands more than one viewing, for images recur like notes in music and the movement backards as well as forwards pulls always towards the present. I am here and here and here. The clock in the old Caledonian station has lost its hands, but a smaller clock suspended on one of its faces continues to record the time. A slow gun salute is firing behind the cars and people and wet pavements of Princes Street with all its Christmas lights on.

* * *

Elizabeth Sussex
(Financial Times, 1970)

na Cornwell comments: "Her style is her own, with its careful exaggerated through reframing – her associative editing, and e pace. It has its own kind of order..."

This page:
Still, *These Walls*
Previous pages:
Tait's information sheets:
Hugh MacDiarmid, A Portrait,
The Leaden Echo and the Golden Echo,
Where I Am is Here

Resources

A page from Tait's photo album

Chronology

1918
11 November, born Margaret
Caroline Tait, Kirkwall,
Orkney, Scotland. Parents
Charles Tait (d.1967) and
Mary Isbister Tait (d.1964),
brothers Maxwell
(1917–1979), William
Isbister (1920–), John
A.S.(1922–1990),
Harald I. (1924–1958).
Family home in Broad
Street, Kirkwall.

1923–1926
Kirkwall primary school.

1924–1954
'Permanent' address,
Buttquoy House, Kirkwall,
school years, university,
war years, post war.

1926–1934
Esdaile School, Edinburgh.

1930s
Taking photographs of
family and friends and
places: Scapa, Eynhallow,
Skaill, Ingsay, Redbanks,
Longhope, Skara Brae,
Yesnaby, Eday, Kirkwall.

1935
Experiments with different
exposure times for several
photographs (interiors, two
self portraits).

1936
Studies medicine at
Edinburgh University. Stays
at 59 North Castle Street,
Blacket Place, Bank Street
and Cambridge Street.

1941
Qualifies in medicine,
MB ChB, at Edinburgh
University.

1943
BSc, Edinburgh University.
Joins the Royal Army
Medical Corps (RAMC),
serves in UK.

1943–1945
Serves in India. Visits
Kashmir, Agra and Delhi.

1945
Serves in Ceylon (Sri
Lanka). Subsequently
compiles photo album of
visits to Kashmir, Agra,
Delhi and Kandy.

1945–1946
Serves in Johore, Malaya,
visits Singapore.

1946
26 March sails for home
from Singapore on the
Winchester Castle.
In Orkney during April.

Visits Adelaide Petersen,
Stavanger, Norway.

Works in Bristol (hospital
duties).

To Edinburgh, living at 46
Ormidale Terrace, where "I
was an ex-service H. (House
Physician) at 'Sick Kids'
(Royal Hospital for Sick
Children)".

1947
Summer holiday in Paris, and then Italy. Visits Florence, Assisi, Perugia, Venice, Como, Milan.

1948
Visits Lake District.

Lives in London staying at 36 Parliament Hill while job hunting.

Works in Shoreditch, lives at 93 Shepherdess Walk.

In the USA. Visits Washington DC (with parents).

July in Orkney.

1948–49
Locum in South of England, including spell as assistant to her uncle's practice in Windlesham, Surrey. Lives at Holly Cottage, School Road, Windlesham.

1949
July / August. Locum in Pontrhydyfen, Glamorgan.

1950
April returns to Perugia. Studies at Università Italiana per Stranieri.

1950–52
Studies film at Centro Sperimentale di Cinematografia, Rome, Italy.

1953
Founds Ancona Films with Peter Hollander, Rome, Italy.

1954
Tenant at 91 Rose Street, Edinburgh (until 1973).

August. The Rose Street Film Festival.

1954–62
Locum, throughout the UK.

1955
August. 2nd Rose Street Film Festival, Edinburgh. Films screened: *Calypso, A Portrait of Ga, Happy Bees, Orquil Burn, The Leaden Echo and the Golden Echo*, by Margaret Tait, *Sometimes a Newspaper*, and *Shapes*, by Peter Hollander, *Affisioni* (Posters) by Luigi Bazzoni and Mario Fenelli.

1959
Lane Furniture, a book of stories, published in Edinburgh.

The Grassy Stories, short stories for children, published in Edinburgh.

Origins and Elements, poems, published in Edinburgh.

1960
Subjects and Sequences, poems, published in Edinburgh.

The Hen and the Bees, poems, published in Edinburgh.

Margaret, Zou Zou and camera

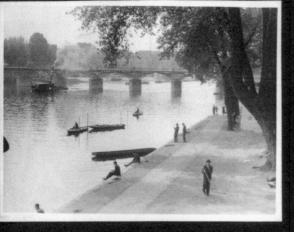

I went to Paris

46 Ormidale Terrace

Seashore

153

1960s
Lives in Edinburgh, East Sutherland, Kirkwall.

1964
A Poet in New York, sequence of pictures based on Lorca's poem is exhibited as a small independent show at 91 Rose Street, during the Edinburgh Festival.

1965
Lives at Slow Bend, Helmsdale, Sutherland (until 1973).

1968
Lives at Buttquoy House (until 1975).

9 December. Marries Alex Pirie.

1970
Retrospective at the 24th Edinburgh International Film Festival.

1972
March. *Umbrella*, vol. 1 no. 2 published by the Richard Demarco Gallery Edinburgh featuring "The Long Light Days of Margaret Tait" by Robert Shure.

1975
Moves to Aith, Sandwick, Orkney.

February. Work exhibited at the First Festival of Independent British Cinema in Bristol.

1975 (continued)
September. Mike Leggett and Annabel Nicolson visit Orkney (Buttquoy House).

"To Anybody At All" included in *Scottish Love Poems, a Personal Anthology*, edited by Antonia Fraser. Canongate, Edinburgh.

1977
Tour of South West England organised by Mike Leggett.

Screening at London Film Makers Co-op.

1978
Spectrum, BBC Scotland arts series, 30-minute programme about her work called *Poet with a Camera*.

1979
Work screened at Third International Festival of Avant-Garde Film, National Film Theatre, London.

Late 1970s to 1990s
A small number of showings at the Pier Arts Centre, Stromness, Orkney.

Aerial, Colour Poems, Place of Work and *Tailpiece*, enter distribution with London Film Makers Co-op (listed in Distribution Supplement no.3) to be joined by *Hugh MacDiarmid, A Portrait* and *Land Makar*.

1982
Work screened at 3rd
International Festival of
Film and Television in the
Celtic Countries, Wexford,
Ireland.

1983
Margaret Tait Film Maker, a
documentary profile,
directed by Margaret
Williams transmitted on
Channel Four Television in
the series *The Eleventh
Hour* on 25 April. Includes
Margaret Tait talking with
Tamara Krikorian.

1984–99
March. Orquil Studio.
A place of work.

1987
9 March. Films by Margaret
Tait transmitted on Channel
Four Television in the series
The Eleventh Hour. Features:
*Hugh MacDiarmid, A
Portrait, A Portrait of Ga,
Colour Poems,* and *Aspects of
Kirkwall: Some Changes.*
Includes interview extracts
from the earlier *Margaret
Tait Film Maker.*

1988
Work included in the
programme *Film Maker as
Poet* (with work by Stan
Brakhage and Bruce Baillie)
presented by David Finch at
the European Media Art
Festival, 1–11 September, in
Osnabruck.

1992
Blue Black Permanent.
Feature film, screenplay and
direction by Margaret Tait.

1993
27 July. Screening at the
National Film Theatre
London of selected short
films.

1994
Lives at Cruan, Firth,
Orkney.

1995
July. Ute Aurand visits
Orkney.

1996
31 May. *A Portrait of Ga,
Where I Am is Here, Aerial,
Colour Poems* and *On the
Mountain* enter distribution
in Germany through Freunde
der Deutschen Kinemathek.
To be joined by *Garden Pieces*
on 3 February 1999.

1998
*Hugh MacDiarmid,
A Portrait* and *Aerial,*
included in the film
programme *Film Poems*
curated by Peter Todd at
the National Film Theatre
London, which subsequently
tours.

1999
16 April. Margaret Tait dies
at home in Firth, Orkney.

4 July. The Lux Cinema,
London, *A Tribute To
Margaret Tait,* film
programme curated by
Peter Todd.

1999 (continued)
Alex Pirie and Alan Watson make a video record (home video) of Orquil Studio before it is emptied.

2000
26 April. The Lux Cinema, London, *Visionary Histories: Maya Deren, Marie Menken, Margaret Tait*, programme curated by Peter Todd.

May. Alex Pirie deposits films and negatives with the Scottish Screen Archive.

October. National Film Theatre, London, retrospective with three programmes of short films: *Places of Work, Land Makar, Film Poems*, and the feature *Blue Black Permanent*, curated by Benjamin Cook and Peter Todd.

2001
Garden Pieces, included in a film touring programme on the theme of the garden, curated by Peter Todd.

2003
Included in *A Century of British Film and Video Artists* at Tate Britain, curated by David Curtis.

2004
Alex Pirie deposits Margaret Tait's papers with the Orkney Archive, Kirkwall.

Scottish Screen Archive receives a grant of £20,000 from the Esmée Fairburn Foundation towards restoring its Margaret Tait film materials.

August. Major retrospective at Edinburgh International Film Festival (18-29 August) with five programmes of short films and the feature *Blue Black Permanent*, curated by Peter Todd.

16 November. Touring programme launched at Cecil Sharp House, London by LUX, of two programmes of films with an accompanying publication, curated by Peter Todd.

Filmography

One is One
1951, 34 mins, black and white, sound
"Made in co-operation with Fernando Birri and Peter
Hollander, all of us students at Centro Sperimentale di
Cinematografia, Rome, at the time." — Margaret Tait

Three Portrait Sketches
1951, 10 mins, black and white, silent
Portraits of Claudia Donzelli, Saulat Rahman and Fernando
Birri.

The Lion, the Griffin, and the Kangaroo
1952, 18 mins, black and white, sound
With Peter Hollander
A documentary film on Perugia and the University for
Foreigners.

A Portrait of Ga
1952, 4.30 mins, colour, sound
An intimate portrait of the film maker's mother.

Happy Bees
1955, 17 mins, colour, sound
"Happy Bees was intended to be an evocation of what it was
like to be a small child in Orkney; when, one (wrongly)
remembers, it was sunny all the time, and everything is
bursting with life. A film about what surrounds a child, so
quite a lot of it is watched at child level." — Margaret Tait

Orquil Burn

1955, 35 mins, colour, sound

"A voyage of exploration, on foot, up the length of an Orkney Burn, a walk which could be done in less than a day, but which, for the film, is spread and apportioned. It's the film maker exploring or re-exploring a burn which she knows quite well, which she has 'always' known but never before gone right to the source of, in the hill. What I found, going upstream, was that while the actual stream of course got narrower and the bridges needed to cross it got smaller and neater (just a plank of wood for the highest one up) the area of wetness – of water lying on the ground and trickling downhill – was wider and wider. I had expected to find 'a source', but it turned out that the sources were many, the origins widespread; and there was no particular point at which I could say 'this is the source of the Orquil burn'." — Margaret Tait

The Leaden Echo and the Golden Echo

1955, 7 mins, colour, sound

"This is an early film of mine – started in 1948, set aside and returned to now and again, and completed in 1955 – in which I tried matching images of my own to the poem of Gerard Manley Hopkins. When it came to editing, I read the poem, for recording first, and the pictures fitted, because I had the relevant lines in mind at the time of shooting; and I think I had to insert only one pause in the pre-recorded track." — Margaret Tait

Calypso

1955, 4 mins, colour, sound

Painted directly on film by Margaret Tait to calypso music.

The Drift Back
1956, 10 mins, black and white sound
A documentary made for Orkney District Council Education
Committee about the return of families to Orkney.

Rose Street
1956, 20 mins, black and white, sound
A film about Rose Street; a road which runs parallel to
Edinburgh's main thoroughfare – Princes Street – in the
heart of the capital's New Town. Tait records the atmosphere
and pace of the streets in shots of shops, pubs and children at
play.

Hugh MacDiarmid, A Portrait
1964, 9 mins, black and white, sound
"A study of the poet, who was 71 at the time. There is
straightforward material, of him in his own home, and, in
addition to speaking his own poems, the poet gracefully
enacts the film maker's interpretation of them. The poems
heard are "You Know Who I Am", "Somersault", "Krang" and
some lines out of "The Kind of Poetry I Want". The music is
Francis George Scott's setting of MacDiarmid's "The Eemis
Stane", sung by Duncan Robertson accompanied on the piano
by Olive Ogston." — Margaret Tait

" ... the poet himself amid all the scenes and objects that
surround his daily life ... and lines of his poems, in his own
voice, echo through the images so that the film speaks out
like music whether or not you have first looked up the
words ... "
— Elizabeth Sussex, *Financial Times*, 9 September 1970

Palindrome
1964, 3 mins, sound
A filmic palindrome with two players (Ron Conway and Stella
Cartwright). Music by Trevor Duncan (Boosey and Hawkes
recording).

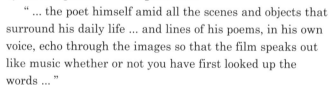

Where I Am is Here

1964, 35 mins, black and white, sound

"Starting with a six-line script (in 1963), which just noted down a kind of event to occur, and recur, my aim was to construct a film with its own logic, its own correspondences within itself, its own echoes and rhymes and comparisons, through close exploration of the everyday, the commonplace, in the city, Edinburgh, where I stayed at the time. The music, *Hilltop Pibroch*, by Hector MacAndrew, is a setting of my poem of that name, and is performed by Hector himself, on the fiddle, and by music hall singer Lilane (Lilian Gunn) who accompanies herself on the piano accordion. The seven titles within the film are: *Complex, Here and Now, Interlude, Crocodile, Come and See This, Out of this World, The Bravest Boat*." — Margaret Tait

"*Where I Am is Here* has none of the obvious shots of Edinburgh, and a cold, sad, essentially Scottish strangeness: the dream of a city as it flows in the bloodstream of the people who live in it. Scripted, photographed and edited by Margaret Tait, its superb and intricate construction demands more than one viewing, for images recur like notes in music and the movement backwards as well as forwards pulls always towards the present. I am here and here and here."

— Elizabeth Sussex, *Financial Times*, 9 September 1970

The Big Sheep

1966, 41 mins, black and white, sound

A journey through the Highlands where echoes of the clearances, of 'handed-down memories', still affect people.

"Part One, tourists are carried north, coach load after coach load; and here is the countryside they come to see, dotted with sheep continually cropping the grass and whin. Then – after the lamb sales – the lambs are carried south, float after float.

Part Two, and the seaboard life of today; the railway line along the very edge of a sandy coast, school sports near the salmon river, crofters' fields where the Cheviot sheep now figure, local buses, electricity, Highland Games and the pibroch contest. John N. MacAskill plays the *Lament for Donald Of Laggan*. A small burn tumbles endlessly seaward, sometimes quietly, sometimes in spate, and the film searches the same few yards of its length again and again, watching the swirl of water, in the company of the coalman who could listen to that sound forever." — Margaret Tait

" ... patterns are all evolving around sheep and busloads of tourists, children running up and down the little space between the pens at a sheep auction. Then behind some political and army recruiting posters pinned on trees, a single line rings out in a mellifluous Highland voice: "Why don't you get your sheep to go and fight for you?" Sheep occupy deserted cottages, but people increasingly emerge: school sports, Highland games embodying what remains of a whole culture, a 15-minute pibroch lament bravely sustained through a marvellous succession of images of life going on – life with the sheep, the telephone, electricity; life as continuous as river water in ebb or spate. The 40-minute film makes considerable demands on anyone reluctant to have his imagination put into play." — Elizabeth Sussex, *Financial Times*, 9 September 1970

Splashing

1966, 6 mins, sound

Action improvised by Paul Tait, Ian Pirie, Marion Pirie.

A Pleasant Place

1969, 21 mins, sound

"Evokes the feelings of a marriage from which the passion has inexplicably drained out."

— Elizabeth Sussex. *Financial Times*, 9 September 1970.

He's Back (The Return)

1970, 20 mins, sound

Jake Foubister, a scientist, returns home after a period of imprisonment in a foreign country.

John Macfadyen (The Stripes in the Tartan)

1970, 3.30 mins, colour, sound

Painted directly on to film "Made over the same period of time and similar methods to *Painted Eightsome*, the music being entitled, *John Macfadyen*, a march tune." — Margaret Tait

Painted Eightsome

1970, 7 mins, colour, sound

"An eightsome reel played by Orkney Strathspey and Reel Society, recorded in about 1955–56 later transferred to 35mm optical track with clear picture and gradually painted, over the years. Eights of different things – figures, antlers, or sometimes just blobs in tartan colours – dance their way through the figure of the reel." — Margaret Tait

Aerial

1974, 4 mins, colour, sound

"Touches on elemental images: air, water (and snow), earth, fire (and smoke), all come into it. The track consists of a drawn out musical sound, single piano notes and some neutral sounds. The picture is a colour print from an original which is partly in colour and partly in black and white."

— Margaret Tait

Colour Poems

1974, 12 mins, colour, sound

"Nine linked short films. Memory, chance observation, and the subsuming of one in the other. The titles within the film are: *Numen of the Boughs, Old Boots, Speed Bonny Boat, Lapping Water, Incense, Aha, Brave New World, Things, Terra Firma.* A poem started in words is continued in images – Part of another poem as an addition to the picture – Some images formed by direct-on-film animation – Others 'found' by the camera." — Margaret Tait

On the Mountain

1974, 32 mins, black and white / colour, sound

"There's a film within a film, here. A film called *Rose Street* is enclosed, intact with academy leader, censor's certificate and credit and end titles, inside a picture of the street in 1973, to make together, *On the Mountain.* Rose Street, Edinburgh, is a street I knew well in all the years that Ancona Films had premises there. I saw it changing from being a place of over-crowded tenements, children playing in the street, pubs and small shops serving people who lived there, among others, into a pedestrian precinct with trendy boutiques and blocks of offices." — Margaret Tait

These Walls

1974, 6.30 mins, black and white / colour, silent

From the same year as *On the Mountain* with many of the same places filmed but with a focus on the walls, with photographs and pictures up, of Tait's Rose Street base.

Place of Work
1976, 31 mins, colour, sound
"A close study of one garden and house and what could be
seen there and heard there within the space of time from
June 1975 to November 1975. An evocation of a place (in
Orkney) with lifelong associations, and latterly used as a
work place. A family home, from which at the time of filming,
the family had long gone. My own home in childhood and off
and on through the years, eventually returned to and worked
in (and on). Filmed in the months before leaving it.

The scheme followed, as the film built up, was to take you
from the work table, out the front door, and round the house
in an east south, west and north circling; showing the shape
of the garden; and then to repeat this circle, with excursions
in and out of the house, observing on the way with equal gaze
the creatures in the garden, human activity outside the
glimpses of town, sea and other islands beyond. Into this
come some, in a sense rather obvious, observations about
flowers budding, flowering, turning into pods and being
shaken and broken by the wind. As the trees are battered
bare, we return to the editing bench, overhearing that the
telephone is to be left connected 'until Monday'."
— Margaret Tait

Tailpiece
1976, 10 mins, black and white, sound
"The film was conceived as a coda to a longer (colour) film,
Place Of Work, made in the same year. It covers the time of
finally emptying a longtime family home, with its personal
memories and connection with some of my own work.
Fragments of verse (from Lorca's *Poet in New York*), along
with young children's voices released into the emptying rooms
and staircases, and an ersatz "pop" music track, clarify the
familiar and the alien in the situation." — Margaret Tait

Aspects of Kirkwall: Shape of a Town
1977, 10 mins, colour, sound
Part of *Aspects of Kirkwall*, Tait's series of films about the
changing townscape of Tait's hometown. "What exactly has
changed, in living memory, – 'nothing', or 'mainly the shops',
or 'everything'?" — Margaret Tait

Aspects of Kirkwall: Occasions
1977, 10 mins, colour, sound
Part of a series of films about the changing townscape of
Kirkwall, looking in particular at special events in the town.
These include the Orkney Agricultural Society County Show,
a boat race, and the Remembrance Day parade.

Aspects of Kirkwall: The Ba', over the Years
1981, 65 mins, black and white / colour, sound
Part of a series of films about the changing townscape of
Kirkwall. This film was filmed between 1954 and 1980 at the
Ba', a traditional annual ball game which takes place through
the town.

Aspects of Kirkwall: Some Changes
1981, 22 mins, colour, sound
"Changes in appearance and in emphasis in the town of
Kirkwall in recent years. Marchers in protest demonstration
walk silently to the Islands Council offices, as a group of
officials with briefcases arrives (on the day of a Public Inquiry
into the refusal of planning permission for test drilling
uranium in Orkney). 'No Uranium' stickers abound. In the
end of the film, the BBC is there in considerable presence, on
the Kirk Green in front of the cathedral, to record a
programme inviting public comment on the uranium issue.
The traditional curfew bell (the 'eight o'clock bells') and a
lullaby accompany their packing up at the end of the
evening's work."
— Margaret Tait

Aspects of Kirkwall: The Look of the Place

1981, 18 mins, black and white, sound

Part of a series of films subtitled "a related group of townscapes ... The film, which was finally completed in April 1981, aims physically to describe the town as it eventually became, using material filmed between 1969 and 1976 ... Spoken comments are few. Sounds of the place accompany the look of it. The whistling *The Streets of Laredo* (or perhaps an older tune on which that is based) echoes through the streets like something much more ancient." — Margaret Tait

Land Makar

1981, 32 mins, colour, sound

"This is a landscape study of an Orkney croft, with the figure of the crofter, Mary Graham Sinclair, very much in the picture. The croft is West Aith, on the edge of a small loch, which almost every passing visitor stops to photograph or draw or paint. I have been filming this beautiful place since 1977, observing many of the human activities which alter and define how it looks. The croft is worked in the old style, and has unfenced fields, tethered animals and flagstone roofs. Mechanised aids are brought in when appropriate, but much is done by one woman's labour. The film is constructed so that the sequences are like a number of canvases. The film is divided into seasons, starting with harvest, a hard-won harvest, as the black-and-white sequence suggests. Nevertheless, the oats look golden and beautiful when standing in stooks of sheaves. Then we look at some other winter stores, accompanied by Mary Sinclair talking about how people in Orkney used to grow much more. Winter is suggested by the glowing fire indoors and the ice on the loch; the day of spring ploughing is still rather bitter. We then see the sudden burst into summer, with flowers everywhere, and Mary Sinclair tells of the many birds nesting and hatching on her land.

She inspects the nest of a swan at the lochside (telling how she gave the swan some help in the building of the nest).

Land Makar (continued)

An evening view of the landscape accompanies Mary
Sinclair's account of her yearly midsummer walk with a
friend (up the hillside in the background). Then there's the
hay harvest, a long spell of communal work; and, after one
haystack is blown down in a gale, the rebuilding of the stack.
By this time it's autumn again, the swan's family has grown
up, and the fields are much more bare. In the long shadows of
a winter afternoon, Mary Sinclair carries a sack of grass she
has just cut from the meadow, and lays it down at the door of
her barn; then she feeds her hens, and talks about them. The
film ends with a brown winter landscape and the sound of
Whooper Swans, winter visitors which were also heard in the
winter stores sequence at the beginning of the film."
— Margaret Tait
Note: Makar is a Scots word, meaning poet.

Blue Black Permanent

1992, 86 mins, colour, sound

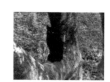

Tait's debut feature is about a daughter's attempts to come to
terms with her mother's death, not only through examining
her own childhood memories but also going back further in
time, to tales of her mother's own childhood. Its structure is
filled with flashbacks and dreams.

Garden Pieces

1998, 12 mins, colour, sound

"Garden Pieces is a set of three pieces. *Round The Garden* is
literally a look right round a back garden, from a central
point, repeated *da capo*. As a garden, it's a place of
potentiality still, but it is a place all right. *Fliers* is an
animated piece, scratched-on. With added dyes. *Grove*, the
longest of the three, studies and contemplates a group of trees
planted maybe 60 years ago in a disused quarry. An original
score by John Gray, written with that very grove in mind, will
provide the music for all three pieces. The music is to have
equal prominence with the picture." — Margaret Tait

Garden Pieces (continued)

"Looking at these (Garden) pieces again tonight, see the beachcomber artist, the searching experimental spirit, so quintessentially Margaret, and a poignant sense of her own mortality: the camera circles round a summer garden, lush with life, seeking shadows within the light, pausing momentarily as it passes over an empty chair."
— Gerda Stevenson, *The Orcadian*, 17 May 1999.

Grove
Is a holy place
Calmly looked at for what it is.
It is as it should stay.
Although of course
Nothing and nowhere stays as it is
So that the particular time
of the grove being seen –
our view of it, the feeling about it,
and the sound heard there
all have a
there and then and never again quality.
— Margaret Tait, February 1998

This filmography was produced from a number of sources including information and publicity sheets produced by Margaret Tait, from information held by LUX and Scottish Screen Archive. On publicity Ancona Films is often listed as the production company and sometimes production credits say 'Script, camera, edited, produced, directed by Margaret Tait while others say 'Film' 'Filmed' or 'by' Margaret Tait. It is an initial filmography in terms of the details that might emerge as the films are restored and the papers catalogued. More detail on credits for the films can be found from some of the sources quoted in the resources section. Nearly all the films listed are on 16mm film. It would appear that four films are lost. They are *Palindrome*, *Splashing*, *He's Back (The Return)* and *A Pleasant Place*.

Bibliography

By Margaret Tait
Lane Furniture: A Book of Stories,
(Edinburgh: M.C. Tait, 1959).
Origins and Elements, poems,
(Edinburgh: M.C. Tait, 1959). Cover by Peter Hollander.
The Grassy Stories: Short Stories for Children,
(Edinburgh: M.C. Tait, 1959).
The Hen and the Bees: Legends and Lyrics, poems,
(Edinburgh: M.C. Tait, 1960). Cover by Robin Philipson.
Subjects and Sequences, poems,
(Edinburgh: M.C. Tait, 1960).
"Films by Margaret Tait", statement,
Time Out, No.22. 18 April 1980, p.45.
"George Mackay Brown Remembered",
Chapman, No.84, 1996, pp.33–34.
"Film-poem or poem-film: A Few Notes about Film and Poetry",
Poem Film Film Poem, No.2, November 1997, pp.4–5.
"Garden Pieces, Their Slow Evolution",
Poem Film Film Poem, No.5, December 1999, pp.1–3.

On Margaret Tait
Aurand, Ute, "Margaret Tait", *Margaret Tait Film Tour*
programme brochure, (Berlin: Ute Aurand, 1994).
Aurand, Ute, "Die Filmpoetin Margaret Tait ist gestorben",
Film, No.6, 1999, pp.4–5.
Bell, Gavin, "A Reel Visionary",
Scotsman, 27 September 2000, p.14.
Brown, George Mackay, on *Hugh MacDiarmid, A Portrait,*
Orcadian, 13 December 1979.
Burch, Noel, "Narrative / Diegesis – Thresholds, Limits",
Screen, Vol.23 No2, July–August 1982, pp.30–31.
Cook, Ben, and Todd, Peter, "Margaret Tait", National Film
Theatre programme booklet, October 2000, pp.34–35.
Crichton, Torcuil, "Film Honour for Orkney's Movie Poet",
Sunday Herald (Glasgow), 17 September 2000, p.10.
Curtis, David, "Britain's Oldest Experimentalist ... Margaret
Tait", *Vertigo,* No.9, Summer 1999, pp.62–63.

Elley, Derek, "Blue Black Permanent", review,
Variety, 14 December 1992, p.47.

Fabig, Monika, "A Report About Women Film makers in
Independent Film – Germaine Dulac, Maya Deren, Margaret
Tait", (Hamburg: Monika Fabig), unpublished 1987.

Film User, "A Portrait of Ga", review, *Film User*,
Vol.9 Issue 100. February 1955, p.108,

Film User, "The Drift Back", review, *Film User*,
Vol.11, Issue 130, August 1957, p.340.

Finch, David, "Film-Maker as Poet", European Media Art
Festival (1–11 September) catalogue, Osnabruck, 1988.

French, Philip, "Blue Black Permanent",
Observer, 4 April 1993, p.54.

Gough-Yates, Kevin, "Moving Pictures",
Art Monthly, June 1983, p.33.

Grigor, Murray, "The Films of Margaret Tait", 24th Edinburgh
International Film Festival brochure, 1970, pp.52–54.

Grigor, Murray, "Margaret Tait", obituary,
Independent, 12 May 1999, p.6.

Hammond, Wally, "Blue Black Permanent", review,
Time Out, 31 March–7 April 1993, p.54.

Hunter, Allan, note on production of *Blue Black Permanent*,
Screen International, No.862, 19 June 1992, pp.20–21.

Isaacs, Jeremy, *Storm Over 4: A Personal Account*, (London:
Weidenfeld and Nicholson, 1989), p.173.

Johnston, Sheila, "Blue Black Permanent", review,
Independent, 2 April 1993, p.16.

Krikorian, Tamara, "On the Mountain and Land Makar:
Landscape and Townscape in Margaret Tait's Work",
Undercut, No.7/8, Spring 1983, pp.17–19.

Leggett, Mike, "The Autonomous Film-Maker: Margaret Tait
Films and Poems 1951–76", unpublished article, 1979.

Leggett, Mike, "On the Mountain", review,
Time Out, No.522. 18 April 1980, p.45.

Leggett, Mike, "Margaret Tait", *A Directory of British Film
and Video Artists*, ed. Curtis, David (Luton: John Libby
Media / London: Arts Council of England, 1996), pp.190–192.

Le Grice, Malcolm, "First Festival of Independent British Cinema", *Studio International*, Vol.189, No.975, May–June 1975, p.225.

McKibbin, Tony, "Scottish Cinema: A Victim Culture", *Cencrastus*, No.73, 2002, p.29.

Macneacail, Aonghas, "Primula Scotia at Yesnaby (for Margaret Tait: 1918–1999.)", poem, *Orcadian*, 17 May 1999.

Malcolm, Derek, "Blue Black Permanent", review, *Guardian*, 1 April 1993, p.5.

Maxford, Howard, "Blue Black Permanent", review, *What's On In London*,7 April 1993, p.35.

Moir, Jan, "First Person Highly Singular", *Guardian*, 31 March 1993, pp.8–9.

Nairn, Edward, "Stills from Orquil Burn and Happy Bees", poem, 2nd Rose Street Film Festival leaflet, August, 1955.

Orcadian, The "Three Jubilee Film Shows", *Orcadian*, 22 September 1977.

Petrie, Duncan, *Screening Scotland*, (London: British Film Institute, 2000), pp.164–5, p.168.

Pirie, Alex, (complied by) "Margaret Tait Film Maker 1918–1999: Indications Influence Outcomes", *Poem Film Film Poem*, No.6, 2000, pp.1–12.

Redding, Judith M. and Victoria Brownworth, "Margaret Tait", *Film Fatales*, (Seattle: Seal Press), pp.109–111.

Reyner, J. L., "Margaret Tait" in *Edinburgh Excerpts*, *Continental Film Review*, November 1970, p.9.

Reynolds, Lucy, "Colour Poems" in the programme notes for Film Poems 4: Messages, touring programme, doubles as *Poem Film Film Poem*, No.12, September 2003, pp.6–7.

Sandhu, Sukhdev, "Unique Vision of a Film Poet", *Daily Telegraph*, 23 August 2004, p.17.

Shure, Robert, "The Long Light Days of Margaret Tait", *Umbrella*, published by Richard Demarco Gallery, Vol.1 No.2, March 1972.

Smith, Ali, "Margaret Tait", LUXONLINE tour, www.luxonline.org.uk, 2004.

Sparrow, Felicity, "Garden Pieces" in the programme notes for Garden Pieces a single screen touring programme on the theme of the Garden, doubles as *Poem Film Film Poem*, No.9, February 2001, pp.1–2.

Stevenson, Gerda, "Margaret Tait", obituary,
Scotsman, 5 May 99.

Stevenson, Gerda, "The Late Margaret Tait, Film Maker – An
Appreciation", *Orcadian*, 17 May 1999.

Sussex, Elizabeth, "Margaret Tait, film-maker",
Financial Times, 9 September 1970.

Sussex, Elizabeth, "Margaret Tait", obituary,
Guardian, 13 May 1999, p.22.

Today's Cinema, "Experimental Film Magazine in Orkneys",
Today's Cinema, Vol.88, Issue 7765, 30 April 1957, p.4.

Todd, Peter, "The Margaret Tait Project", *Media Education
Journal*, Issue 33, Spring, 2003, pp.27–30.

Todd, Peter, "Margaret Tait", LUXONLINE essay,
www.luxonline.org.uk, 2004.

Todd, Peter (compiled by), "Remembering Margaret Tait
(1918–1999) A Deeper Knowledge Than Wisdom",
contributions from Ute Aurand, Annabel Nicolson, Peter
Todd (version of LUXONLINE essay), Sarah Wood and the
'script' *Video Poems for the 90s* by Margaret Tait,
Vertigo, Vol.2, No.7 Autumn / Winter 2004, pp.53–55.

The Times, "Margaret Tait", obituary, 28 May 1999, p.31.

Winn, Joss, "Preserving The Hand-Painted Films of Margaret
Tait", MA dissertation, University of East Anglia, Norwich,
2002, unpublished.

Yates, Robert, "Blue Black Permanent", review, *Sight and
Sound*, April 1993, p.43.

The papers of Margaret Tait include photocopies of articles
she often used for publicity purposes (often from the Scottish
press) on flyers or sheets which do not always have dates or
sources. Hopefully these will be identified, sourced, and dated
as cataloguing and research is undertaken.

Resources

Papers

AHRB British Artists' Film and Video Study Collection at
Central Saint Martins, University of the Arts, London
Includes letters, interviews and publicity sheets.
www.studycollection.org.uk

bfi National Library, London
Includes articles in film journals and newspaper articles.
www.bfi.org.uk

LUX, London
Includes publicity sheets and articles.
www.lux.org.uk

National Library of Scotland, Edinburgh
Correspondence in the MacDiarmid Collection.
www.nls.uk

Orkney Archive, Kirkwall, Orkney
The major collection of Tait's papers relating to her films.
www.orkney.gov.uk

Scottish National Gallery of Modern Art, Edinburgh
Correspondence in the Richard Demarco archive dating from
the 1970s.
www.natgalscot.ac.uk

Scottish Screen Archive, Glasgow
Correspondence between Tait and the Films of Scotland
committee 1955–78.
www.scottishscreen.com

Films

bfi, London
Distributes the feature film *Blue Black Permanent*, while the archive holds copies of the two Channel Four television programmes of Margaret Tait films.
www.bfi.org.uk

Freunde der Deutschen Kinemathek, Berlin
Distribution collection of selected films.
www.fdk-berlin.de

LUX, London
Distribution collection of selected films and touring exhibition.
www.lux.org.uk

Scottish Screen Archive, Glasgow
The major collection of Tait's films and film materials.
www.scottishscreen.com

South London Poem Film Society (c/o LUX)
Distribution collection of selected films.
www.lux.org.uk

Contributors

Ute Aurand is a film maker based in Berlin.

Benjamin Cook is director of LUX.

David Curtis is Senior Research Fellow at Central Saint Martins, University of the Arts, London, where he runs the AHRB British Artists' Film and Video Study Collection. He was formerly Senior Visual Arts Officer at the Arts Council of England, with responsibility for artists' film and video.

Gareth Evans is a freelance writer and independent film programmer. He works on the film pages of *Time Out London* and edits the film magazine *Vertigo*. He is a programme advisor to The London Film Festival and Brief Encounters International Short Film Festival, and has served on festival juries across Europe. He is also a director of the new LUX organisation.

Janet McBain is the founding Curator of the Scottish Screen Archive where she has responsibility for the national moving image collection for Scotland. She is the author of articles and essays on aspects of Scottish film production history.

Lucy Reynolds is an artist, writer and film programmer.

Alan Russell has been the Preservation and Technical Officer at the Scottish Screen Archive since 1985. He manages the conservation programme for the Margaret Tait Film Collection and is a member of the British Kinematograph Sound and Television Society (BKSTS).

Ali Smith is a writer. Her most recent novel is *Hotel World* (Penguin 2002) and her most recent collection of short stories is *The Whole Story and Other Stories* (Penguin 2004).

Peter Todd's work includes the films *Diary* and *For You* and the curated touring programmes *Film Poems* (1–4), and *Garden Pieces*.

Sarah Wood is a film maker and film programmer.

Credits

Editors: Peter Todd and Benjamin Cook
Design: Sarah Wood
LUX: Benjamin Cook, Bernhard Frankel, Lyn French,
Jackie Holt, Mike Sperlinger

Thanks:
Alex Pirie, Sarah Christian
Scottish Screen Archive: Janet McBain, Alan Russell,
Adrienne Wilson, Ann Beaton, Alan Docherty
Arts Council England: Sara Bowler, Gary Thomas
Scottish Screen: Alan Knowles
Pier Arts Centre: Andrew Parkinson, Neil Firth
Edinburgh International Film Festival:
Shane Danielsen, Nicola Pierson
National Film and Television Archive: Jerry Rodgers, Brian
Pritchard, Joss Winn, Kieron Webb, Joao Socrates De Oliveira
Haghefilm Laboratories: Juan Vrijs
Martin Sawyer Sound Services
To the venues that have supported the project so far:
Cinematheque Brighton / Michael Sippings
Phoenix Leicester / Alan Alderson-Smith
Broadway Nottingham / Caroline Hennigan
Bristol Watershed / Mark Cosgrove
Dartington Arts / Colin Orr
Thanks for work on bibliography to Alice Fraser and for work
on design to Bridget Hannigan and Woodrow Phoenix.

Photographs in the Margaret Tait collection appear
courtesy of Peter Todd and LUX, with thanks to Jeanette
Sutton for scanning. Film scans from Margaret Tait films
appear courtesy of Scottish Screen Archive. Ownership and
rights of the films and film materials of Margaret Tait, her
poems, stories, papers, and her photographs are held by Alex
Pirie and appear here by kind permission.

LUX

Subjects and Sequences: a Margaret Tait reader is
published on the occasion of a film touring exhibition
organised by LUX with newly restored prints by the Scottish
Screen Archive. See www.lux.org.uk for more details.
Supported by Arts Council England, Scottish Screen, Esmée
Fairburn Foundation and Pier Arts Centre, Orkney.

SCOTTISH
SCREEN